THE TIDY CLOSET

TIPS FROM A FRENCH WOMAN

EASY STEPS AND MOTIVATION TO DECLUTTER YOUR CLOSET AND ORGANISE YOUR WARDROBE

By Marie-Anne Lecoeur

Table of Contents

INTRODUCTION

If you have bought this book, it is probably because, like millions of women out there, you have an overflowing closet and you need some help. For various reasons, time being the one most mentioned, untidiness has taken over your life. You fear that, if you don't do something soon, your closet, bedroom, home and life will be overrun by this all-pervading mess. It didn't happen overnight but over time, and now you are overwhelmed. You may have tried to tidy up before. But, the same thing happens over and over again; after a good, thorough clean up, the mess returns. You have given up. You may begin to worry that you are a hoarder. A lack of motivation and knowledge of where to start and how to tackle the problem stops you in your tracks. You are paralysed into inaction. The situation is getting worse by the day. Dressing chic becomes subordinate to just finding something, anything, to wear. It is easy to let things go, but it takes discipline to put things away in their proper place. Things have a way of getting messy without you noticing.

Before you realise it, you are back to your untidy ways:

- A pair of shoes gets thrown into the closet
- The lid of a shoe box goes missing
- A blouse has fallen off its hanger
- A carefully stacked pile of sweaters topples over
- One shirt gets draped over another on the same hanger
- Belts get shoved in between shelves
- Scarves are scrunched up and tossed into drawers

- Your closet has become the repository for everything and anything.

Does this sound familiar?

Before you know it, your whole bedroom is in complete disarray. Half a dozen outfits, both worn and unworn, lie in a heap on a chair. Dirty laundry is scattered on the floor and you have to scrabble under the bed to retrieve pairs of shoes.

You make excuses, you call them 'reasons', for not tidying up:

- Lack of time
- Over committed
- No help
- Not your job
- Not in your horoscope.

The mess can be overwhelming, especially if left to fester for days, weeks or even months. However, coming up with excuses and burying your head in the sand will not help. To get started, you are going to have to bite the bullet. Drawing from my life in France, this book gives you advice and tips to help you throughout.

In Chapter 1, discover the psychology behind clutter and what makes you do what you do. Learn the differences between a clutterer and a hoarder. Which are you? The reasons for your clutter will be discussed and there will be exercises for you to complete.

In Chapter 2, we shall examine your current situation and sum it up. You may feel cluttered in more ways than one, but help is at hand. Find out how the Pareto Principle relates to your closet and how a lack of motivation has enabled the situation to endure.

In Chapter 3, I lay out all the disadvantages of clutter, and believe me, there are lots. You will wonder why you have put up with the stress when you discover the many ways an untidy closet can affect your life.

Chapter 4 will show you the benefits of a tidy closet. Savings of time, money and space, discovering old favourites whilst bringing in positive energy and leaving you better dressed are the benefits you will reap by decluttering.

In Chapter 5, I shall do my utmost to motivate you to start decluttering. This is often the most difficult step. Once you are past this point, it's all fun and downhill. Being active and not dithering, whilst keeping the consequences of clutter in mind can help. Discover a powerful tool to help you get and stay motivated. Friends and rewards can spur you to a clutter-free zone.

In Chapter 6, you will follow the easy steps that you need to take, to render the decluttering process simple and effective. The eleven steps set out in detail what you need to do, from emptying through cleaning to sorting.

Chapter 7 explores storage concepts. Give yourself free rein to design the closet of your dreams, by unleashing your creativity.

In Chapter 8, find out how to organise your clothes to their and your best advantage. From clothes to lingerie to shoes, there are ideal ways to keep all items. Know which is best to maintain your clothes and your sanity in good condition.

In Chapter 9, you will learn how to keep up the good work so that you don't fall back into old habits. The tidy closet is yours, Madame!

Finally, I have given you a whole bonus chapter, at number 10. This sets out the essential and classic clothes you cannot be without, if you want your wardrobe to work for you and your lifestyle. There is nothing better than having a closet stocked with the very best you can find and afford. You will feel so proud of yourself.

Peppered throughout the book, are easy Tips and Exercises to help you along.

This simple, yet well detailed method will lead you gently, but firmly by the hand, to a well structured wardrobe and a tidy closet. I know how painful it is when you cannot see the wood for the trees, but I am here to help you. Follow the steps and you will find it easy.

So, let's not procrastinate any longer. Let's do this thing. Are you with me? Let's dive right in!

CHAPTER 1

THE PSYCHOLOGY BEHIND CLUTTER

"Have nothing in your house that you do not know to be useful, or believe to be beautiful" – William Morris

If you despair about the mess that you generate every day, you can relax now. You are not alone. You are actually in good company. Studies have shown that 30% of the population are clutterers, whilst only 1% are hoarders.

If you live in the United Kingdom, this 30% represents about 18.6 million people, or in the USA, almost 95 million. We are talking huge numbers here!

This means that about one person in three is a clutter bug, has a messy home, car, bedroom or office desk.

How many clutterers do you know? Does this 30% sound about right to you? I know it is not easy to be sure. Friends, colleagues, acquaintances and even we, do not usually advertise that we are clutterers. We find it too embarrassing. We all like to project an image of being in control and having the perfect home.

Today, however, we can shoo this embarrassment away as we are going to meet the problem head on.

First of all, there is one important issue to decide.

Clutterer Or Hoarder?

Many people fret about whether they are a clutterer or a hoarder. You may feel overwhelmed by your clutter. You may worry you have gone too far and will not be able to clear it all out. Don't despair. The statistics above show that only 1% of the population are hoarders. You are probably just messy and disorganised, that's all. If you can still sleep in your own bed, use your bathroom, kitchen and all your rooms, it means you are not a hoarder. If you don't have to use a machete to hack your way through your corridors, you are not a hoarder. If your relatives are not worried about your disappearance under mountains of junk, you are not a hoarder. You are just in need of a bit of help, that's all. If you are in any doubt, or if you still have lingering worries, then please consult a professional.

Main differences between cluttering and hoarding:

You are a clutterer when you:
- Get overwhelmed with the mess

- Need a reason before tackling the mess

- Find excuses not to deal with untidiness for a while

- Realise you can't find a place to put anything

- Don't make a drama when ditching stuff

- Can't bear to part with some items. If you do, you forget about them quickly

- Stop shopping and acquiring more, once you notice the problem

- Can still have people over but make excuses about the state of the house

- Tidy up eventually

- You bought this book because you want to do something about it.

You are a hoarder when:

- You don't notice the sheer scale of the problem, but everyone else does

- You have duplicates, triplicates or collections of many items

- Your stuff takes over the whole house and beyond

- The problem has escalated over many

years

- The mess takes over your life
- You suffer the social consequences as nobody can visit you
- You have become a recluse
- You find it stressful to ditch even one insignificant item
- You become upset if things get thrown away without your consent
- You have given up your bed to piles of clutter
- The kitchen and bathroom are unusable
- Doorways of your home are blocked
- Your health and safety are at risk
- You may be in debt but still carry on shopping for more
- You have been given this book by a relative but don't know why.

Psychology Of Hoarding

Psychological studies have shown that the areas of the brain which produce strong cravings in addicts, such as smokers and drug users, are associated with conflict and pain. These same areas also show increased activity when hoarders try to decide whether to keep or throw anything away. In order to relieve feelings of anxiety and discomfort, addicts give in to their cravings. Similarly, with hoarders, they decide to keep their items. That pain relief can itself become addictive and so the hoarder keeps on hoarding and the cycle repeats.

Reasons For Cluttering

There are psychological reasons for our cluttering, including depression, anxiety, and just plain fear and procrastination. In extreme cases, these can lead to hoarding. We give many reasons and explanations for keeping things that others can't understand. Let's look at some of them now. Following each reason for cluttering, there is an exercise for you to complete.

Sentimental value

Even if we are not a hoarder, we can get attached to an item and give it sentimental value. The result? We can't bear to throw it out.

On my first trip to the USA, many years ago, I bought an adorable black suede and crochet jacket. One button soon became loose. As I never got around to sewing the button back on, the jacket was unwearable. However, I still didn't want to part with it because it reminded me of that American trip. It didn't matter to me that I never wore it. Finally, the jacket was given away to charity on one of my purges some twenty years later!

Did I regret it? No. The only thing I regretted was not having sewn that button back on so that I could wear the jacket, when it was still fashionable. Silly me. You will not catch me doing this again. (By the way, I never did sew that pesky button back on, but left it in the pocket!).

Exercise

Make a list of things that you never use, but categorically refuse to part with because you've attached some sentimental value to them. Alongside each, write down what it represents to you.

E.g. An old dress = You were wearing it when your husband proposed

A pair of gloves two sizes too small = Used to belong to your grandmother

_____

_____

_____

Due to these sentimental attachments, none of these items are likely to see the inside of a bin or a charity shop.

It is up to you to decide whether or not you wish to part with them. Can you think of other ways to keep the memories alive? You may find that photographs will have the same effect as these mementoes and not take up as much room. Another solution is to store these items away safely in a place where they will not clutter your everyday life. Time to create a memory chest!

Expensive pieces

Even though we have no use for them any longer, we find that we cannot give some pieces away because of the price we paid for them. We feel that we would be throwing money away.

Exercise

Make a list of such pieces now.

E.g. A designer jumpsuit from the 70s
Super high heels that your bunions do not
allow you to wear

_____

_____

_____

Research their current value on auction sites.
If they are still valuable, but you no longer use
them, you can put them up for sale and get
yourself some cold, hard cash. If they are not
worth anything, you have held on to them for
far too long. Donate or ditch!

Financial value in the future

We may hold on to items in the hope that
they will be worth a lot of money in the future
and form part of our children's inheritance.
These items may have absolutely no chance of
ever being worth more than what you paid for

them. In most cases, they will have already lost most, if not all, of their value. However, we do see surprising items achieving some value on television programs like The Antique's Road Show.

A professional dealer may be able to give you an idea of whether any particular item could achieve value in the future.

Exercise

Make a list of your items below that you think may become valuable. Alongside each, write down the value you think they have or might attain.

Old Chanel suit

Vintage Givenchy ball-gown

A Pierre Cardin coat

_____

_____

_____

Now, do some research or consult an antique dealer who specialises in clothes and see if you are right.

With the results to hand, you can then assess

whether they are worth keeping.

Unique

How many of us have objects or clothes that we deem unique and thus irreplaceable? I bet most of us do not even use these, ever. As a matter of fact, they are probably gathering dust at the back of a closet or cupboard as we speak. However, even though we do not ever hold them, admire them or love them, we would rather lose an arm than part with them. Our fear that we would not be able to find anything similar to replace them is what stops us from throwing them away.

Exercise

Write down a list of these pieces that you think are unique.

_____

_____

_____

Now, research these items on your favourite auction site to see if you can find others like them. If you can, they are not unique, so it is time to reassess their place in your closet. If they are truly unique however, isn't it a shame to hide them away? Give them pride of place in your home and enjoy them every day.

Too big a bargain

Another reason (or would that be an excuse?) to hold on to things is that we were savvy or lucky enough to bag something as a bargain and so we figure that we can't let it go. We feel that, if we throw it away, we are somehow throwing away our cleverness or luck. However, bargains come along all the time if you are looking for them.

Exercise

Make a list of these bargain items you can't let go of.

_____

_____

_____

Now, visit charity shops or online stores to see if these pieces are still the same bargain that you think they are. If they are more expensive in the shops, give yourself a pat on the back. If not, reconsider their place in your closet. In the process, you may find even better bargains, just to prove to yourself that you've still got it!

Can't decide where it goes

Some of us can't make a decision as to the rightful place for an object. So the easiest thing for us to do is to keep it and hide it at the back of a drawer.

Someday, you figure, you'll find the perfect place for it.

Exercise

Gather all these misfits together. You may find that some or all of them belong in the categories above. Deal with them accordingly. With the ones that are left, find their rightful place. If you genuinely cannot find a place for them (but not back in the same drawer), do they belong in your home?

You really only ought to keep things that are loved and useful. Everything else is just clutter. Don't let these items take over your home or even worse your life.

What Started The Clutter?

Shopping

You have bought clothes, accessories and shoes indiscriminately over the years. It is tempting to buy into the latest trends. TV adverts, magazines and shops tempt us with more beautiful, glamorous and successful versions of ourselves. We can only become this person, they say, if we buy the latest it-bag, designer dress or shoes. It is difficult to resist this clever, professional marketing.

All our friends have the latest things too. Nobody likes to be the only one not wearing the latest trends.

So how can we resist the BUY BUY BUY ads? The answer is: Change your shopping habits. You'll learn about this as we go along.

I, like other French women, understand the benefits of a simple but classic wardrobe and our buying habits support this. We buy fewer but more versatile clothes of good quality, style and fit. But even I got pulled into buying too much when I first arrived in Britain. After a few years of this buying frenzy, I realised that I had far too many clothes that didn't work for me. That is when I carried out my first purge and regained my French shopping habits. I stick to classics and a pared down wardrobe. Less is more.

Sales

The sales are so hard to avoid. We are led to believe that those purchases are too good to miss, and that we would be fools to pass them by.

We have been brainwashed into viewing those large colourful stickers that scream 'Sales', '30% off' and 'Last Day' as some kind of gospel that means 'Spending now will be your salvation'.

We have been lured into spending on unnecessary and often unwanted items simply because of a bright red sticker. We get hypnotised into a buying frenzy amongst the crowds on sales days, pitched against each other to grab the best bargains. Once you get home though, these plastic and cardboard carrier bags may be shoved into the closet, sometimes without being emptied. The excitement is all gone. You have come out of your shopping trance and now feel a bit guilty or foolish. You are just realising that you have brought in yet more clutter to join the masses of clothes and other stuff already languishing inside your closet. So you end up with less space and more guilt. Don't think that you are alone. Plenty of people do this on a regular basis. It is my opinion that shops and advertisers capitalise on women's primitive instincts to 'gather & collect'. I say that it is high time that we recovered our sense of self and freedom. Let's wake up from the sales trance.

Overwhelmed

When people let a large quantity of things pile up in one area, they find themselves overwhelmed by the situation. It is too much for them to handle and so they feel inclined to turn a blind eye to it. However, the situation can only get worse and it does. Soon, negative feelings of guilt and shame make you stand up and want to do something about it. This is when you need to act and why you have this book.

Excuses

You have given yourself, and possibly the other members of your household, all sorts of excuses as to why you have not yet tackled the mess accumulating in your bedroom and closet.

'Lack of time' is the most used. 'No help' is another. You can fool people for a while and get away with it. However, you cannot fool yourself forever.

You know, both in your conscious and subconscious minds, that these are empty excuses. So, the result is that you end up feeling guilty. You carry this guilt around with you, which does you no good at all. It weighs on your conscience. I know we are only talking about a closet, or a bedroom, but could this be a sign that other areas of your life are neglected too? Perhaps it is time for a re-evaluation.

Exaggerating the problem

The thing with messy areas is that we get easily overwhelmed and stressed out when we think about it. We churn this situation around and around in our mind until we make it out to be much larger than it actually is. By thinking about it over and over instead of dealing with it, we exaggerate the extent of it all. This renders us powerless in our mind to cope and deal with it. The truth is, a closet can be quickly tidied up and sorted out. It is we who make this molehill into a mountain.

Now, let's have a look at your current situation and what your problem really is.

CHAPTER 2

THE SITUATION NOW

"Bottom line is, if you do not use it or need it, it's clutter, and it needs to go." - Charisse Ward

You have been accumulating so much stuff over the years that your closet is bursting at the seams.

The recognition that you have too much in your closet is the first step to doing something about it. You have lived with so many things, for so long, that it has taken until now for you to acknowledge that it is time for change. You have been trying, without any success, to get the motivation you really needed to tackle the task at hand. So far, you have never managed to start, or you have started but never finished. You are a fully paid up member of the Clutter Club!

Now, however:

- You want to turn over a new leaf but don't know where to start

- You are overwhelmed by clutter

- You are discouraged by the mere thought of the huge task ahead of you

- You have less and less room in your closet

- Everything is in disarray

- You have nothing to wear

- Your clothes are always crumpled

- You can't see what you have because it's all crunched together

- You can't see what's lurking at the back of your closet

- You don't wear a large proportion of what you do have

- You have too many different styles of clothes

- Nothing goes with anything

- There are so many different colours, so many different trends

- It's difficult to create an outfit

- You spend a fortune on the wrong clothes.

The Pareto Principle

From personal experience and from what I gather from other women, the Pareto Principle applies to our wardrobe, as well as other areas of life. This means that we wear 20% of our clothes 80% of the time. Consequently, the largest proportion of our wardrobe, or 80%, is hardly ever worn!

Some of this 80% never even sees the light of day and remains unworn since the day it left the shop. Quelle horreur!

The above is true for so many of us. I hold my hand up to this as I used to do it too. But I have seen the light, sister. I now refuse to waste any more of my hard earned cash on clothes that won't earn their keep.

Some women resist paring their wardrobe to a hard core of good quality essentials that will get constant wear. They opt instead to fill their closet with more clothes, but of lower quality, that they hardly use. They are afraid of the 'I have nothing to wear' syndrome and so buy everything. They use the scatter-gun approach to style, 'if I buy everything, some things are bound to go together'. Some use the excuse that they 'don't want to wear the same thing every day' in order to buy more clothes. The reality is that they still wear the same small proportion of their clothes most of the time anyway.

I have found that, the less choice you have, the easier it is to make a decision. You know yourselves if you want an ice cream and the choice is strawberry, chocolate or vanilla, the choice is easy to make. However, try to make a quick decision in an ice cream parlour when faced with dozens of flavours. See? Weren't you just picturing all these tubs of different flavours? Could you make up your mind as to which one to choose? Neither could I.

So you see, the same goes with your clothes.

Believe it or not, you can create just as many different outfits with fewer items than when you are faced with too much choice. With less, you tend to be more adventurous. You will be more willing to try out new combinations instead of always wearing the same top with the same skirt.

The secret is, when you pare down your wardrobe, you must make sure that what you buy goes with as many other pieces as you can. This gives you many combinations and you never look like you wear the same things over and over. We'll talk about this later.

No Motivation

You have reached saturation point. You have had enough. You want change, but you don't know how to do it. You lack motivation and direction. On your own, you know that nothing will happen. Many times before, you have tried to start and finish the decluttering. You tried, in vain, to will yourself through the whole process. However, after a little while, you gave up, either due to outside distractions, children, supper, work or due to giving in and taking the easy way out. So you closed the door behind you and forgot about the whole thing.

It is this lack of motivation that we need to tackle first before we do anything else. We want you buoyed up, energised and ready to go. We want you to jump up and down, figuratively of course, but you can do it literally too if you want.

So come on, join us! Let's get motivated! En avant!

CHAPTER 3

THE DISADVANTAGES OF CLUTTER

"The opposite of simplicity, as I understand it, is not complexity but clutter" - Scott Russell Sanders

Before we can get you motivated, let's see some of the problems that clutter brings into your life. Hopefully, this will help propel you into the motivation mind-set or at least sow the seeds!

Less Room

When you open the doors of your closet, if they can even close at all due to the overfill, you get swept away by the avalanche of stuff. The scale of the untidiness and sheer mountain of clothes make you want to slam the doors and scarper. By having so much, there is less room to move, less space for new clothes and less room to enjoy the clothes you have. In this case, with more and more comes less and less. Soon, your closet is over full and stuff spills out to invade your bedroom floor and surfaces. Every nook and cranny are invaded by more bits and pieces. Your closet and bedroom are in danger of being overtaken by the clutter if you don't do something soon. Things will only go further off-piste if you don't tackle this mess now.

It's A Jumble In There!

You have resorted to throwing things into your closet and closing the door quickly.

Things are so tightly packed that clothes come off hangers when you pull things out.

You don't pick them up because there is nowhere else you could hang them.

Pieces are not coordinated or organised into any set system.

Your shoes are heaped higgledy-piggledy and you find yourself having to dig deep into the pile, every time you need a pair.

Clothes for every season and occasion are crammed together. Thick coats next to light summer jackets, woolly gloves in the midst of summer hats, socks with underwear, scarves interlaced with bikinis.

You reason that, as long as your shoes are not thrown in among your underwear, you are ok. This may happen though, if you don't do something about it soon.

Mistreatment

As we have seen above, your shirts fall down among your shoes and boots and remain there. Every time you fight your way into this pile to retrieve a pair of shoes, your shirts get pulled in all directions, trampled and then buried. They will get dirty, stained and damaged. On shelves, sweaters and tops get mixed together, slide down the back or the sides and end up looking like rags.

Your drawers fare no better and could be even worse. The sock drawer has become more of a sock/tights/underwear/odds and sods drawer. They hardly close, even when you give them a good push with your hip.

You have lost the upper hand. Because clothes are crumpled, you are less likely to wear them. You lack the time or the will to iron them and put them back on the hanger. You are most likely to push them to the back of shelves. The result of all this is that your clothes get damaged and end up having to be thrown away. What a waste of money.

Nothing To Wear

As all your clothes are crushed together and piled high, it is difficult to find anything. Your favourite saying in the morning is "I have nothing to wear." You can't find anything that matches, things have disappeared down the back of your closet, are in piles on the floor or have disappeared altogether. How can you create an outfit with clothes you don't know you have or can't find? It is not realistic.

There is, potentially, plenty to wear in your closet, but not much is ready to wear or wearable. Because they are not well looked after, your clothes are:

- Crumpled and in need of ironing

- Damaged so need to be mended

- Too-old-fashioned and waiting for an 80s revival (fill in your favourite decade here)

- Too small for your current size (10 years ago you used to be a size 6)

- Too young for you

- For different seasons

- For weddings

- Unwearable for many other reasons.

Waste Of Money

Imagine totaling the amount spent on all the clothes and accessories that you have bought blind and hardly worn. That would be about 80% of your wardrobe, as we have seen above. Horrified yet? I am. We could go on a luxurious holiday for that amount. You see, when we buy good quality pieces that match what we've already got, they get worn regularly and for many seasons. They are a worthy investment. The waste is in the money spent on expensive or even cheap clothes, shoes and accessories, that do not get worn. If you don't wear them, it's a waste of money, no matter whether you spent a few pounds or a hundred.

In my book, How To Be Chic and Elegant, I explain in detail the principle of cost per wear. In short, the more you wear a piece, the cheaper it gets with each wear. You may think that you are saving money by buying cheap clothes that will not get worn more than once or twice. However, the opposite is true. You are effectively spending more money than if you buy an expensive but quality item that you will wear for years.

Imagine the money you will save when your wardrobe is organised and tidy. No more futile purchases. No more cheap low quality pieces.

No more maxed out store cards. If you are not going to tidy up and declutter for your style or your sanity, then be a mercenary and do it for the money!

Unnecessary Expense

When you have a social event looming, you prefer to shop for a whole new outfit because you can't face the 'prospect of prospecting' in your closet. So you go to the unnecessary expense of a new dress or separates, shoes, jewellery and handbag.

You do the same thing again for every outing. It is time to stop this cycle, don't you think?

Different Styles

An alien from the planet Zog, looking into your closet, could be forgiven for thinking that your clothes belong to five or six different women. The styles are so different. Because you can't readily see what you own, you are clueless as to, not only what you've got, but what you need. So, when you go shopping, you buy unsuitable and unnecessary pieces. Colours and styles won't match and the whole situation just gets worse and worse.

Fleeting Trends

You buy the latest trends which may be neon colours this season, bohemian skirts the next. When you get home, these will look out of sync with the other pieces you have. You can't create an outfit because, instead of essentials and classics, all you have is trendy pieces that do not go together. You may wear them once or twice at the most. Plenty won't get worn at all.

Trendy pieces, by their very nature, don't last for long. They will, thus, clutter your closet. They will remain unworn and will hinder you from creating outfits that truly work for you and your lifestyle.

Exile

The fact is, you spend less and less time in your bedroom or closet because there is less room and less enjoyment for you. You feel exiled from your once beloved sanctuary. You used to spend hours gazing and touching your clothes, putting together outfits, trying on shoes. These sweet times are sadly long gone. It is no longer a happy experience. Now, when you walk into your bedroom, you are assailed by the mess. Clothes hang all over the place or have fallen on the floor, lying there in a heap, unloved and un-cherished. Shoes are strewn everywhere, one shoe here, one shoe there, mixed with belts, scarves and dirty underwear. It is not a pretty sight. It is enough to make anybody run away in despair. So you do.

Frustration

Surrounded by mess, you may start to panic, especially in the morning when time is of the essence. You ask yourself whether you have enough time to forage through your heaps of messy clothes and put an outfit together. If, every morning, you have to spend a half hour searching for each item, it is no wonder you end up frazzled before you even start your day. The sheer frustration of not finding what you are looking for should not be underestimated. It follows you through the day and taints everything you do.

Stress

We are bombarded every minute of the day with visual, auditory and olfactory stimuli. TV, radio, newspapers, magazines, adverts everywhere, cars driving past, people talking, various machines making noises, exhaust fumes, fast food joints and everything else assault our senses every day. Phew! The mind cannot relax amid this multi-sensory overload. The same can occur within our own homes. People find that they are more relaxed in a tidy room than in a messy one. This cannot come as a surprise to anyone. In a messy room, there is so much clutter that our eyes don't know where to rest. As a result, the mind is over-loaded and it's impossible to be calm. All of the above, frustration, lack of space, waste of time and money, add up to create more and more stress for you, every day. Stress is the one thing that we can all do without.

From the above, you can understand how a messy closet can adversely affect your health. I hope that you are beginning to feel that you want to make changes in your life and your closet. From the problems with messy, let's now see the benefits of tidy. Those little seeds of motivation need a good watering.

CHAPTER 4

THE BENEFITS OF A TIDY CLOSET

"If your house is full of stuff, all the blessings that could fill your house can't get in. The stuff takes over."- Peter Walsh

This chapter is all about the advantages of a tidy closet and the wonderful benefits that it can bring. Let's see how much easier your life could be.

Focus

When the inside of your closet has more in common with a jumble sale, after the mad rush, than a Harrods' display, it is a rather daunting task to focus on what is wearable. You cannot spot anything of value when too many items are fighting for your attention. By decluttering, you will weed out all the obsolete pieces and keep only those that you love, that fit and suit your figure, your shape, that are seasonal, classic and of good quality. This sorting out will enable you to keep less stuff in the same space. By having less to focus on, your eyes will find it easier to locate pieces that can be put together for a great outfit. Less to focus on means better results.

Time Is Precious

When your closet is cluttered, you have to spend more time finding the right clothes.

Sometimes, after having found an item, you discover that a button is missing or a seam has unraveled. Whether you choose to mend it, leave it aside for 'later' or put it back in your closet, it is still a waste of time. You spend extra time putting together an outfit, looking for things, ironing clothes again, repairing them or getting changed two or three times. So much of your precious time is wasted due to lack of organisation. However, when things are tidy, you spend less time looking for items to create an outfit. Additionally, as your clothes are well ordered and cared for, they don't need mending or re-ironing.

Calm

Just thinking of your messy drawers is probably enough to send you into a tailspin. Imagine how calm and satisfied you would feel if, when you opened the door of your closet, your gaze was met with well arranged and sorted clothes. Very calm and satisfied, I would venture. This feeling can set you up in a great mood for the rest of the day. Neatness has the power to calm your mind and help you relax. When your eyes and mind are faced with order and organisation, frustration is replaced by calm.

Money

Imagine how much money you will save once you have decluttered and sorted your wardrobe. You will instantly know what clothes you have. No more money wasted on duplication. No more buying ultra-trendy pieces that will not go with anything else.

Develop a more discerning attitude in the buying process and your money will go further.

Less Is More

Once you have removed all the undesirables from your closet, a more manageable quantity of clothes will be left. Once this is done, you will instantly see what you have and what you need to create your outfits. This works so well for me that I can create an outfit by just thinking about it and visualising what I have. I create my outfits in my mind either before going to bed, in the shower, or on waking. Even with my eyes closed!

Want to wear your new red top today? See in your mind the skirts or trousers that would go well with it. Then move on to the jacket and shoes. Et voilà!

It is easier for you to remember what hangs in your closet when you have less. If you have a large quantity of things, you would not be able to plan your outfit in your mind. This works well for me and lets me utilise my time in an efficient way.

Tidy And Happy

I don't know about you, but, after I have tidied up and cleaned, I feel great. I love to admire the fruits of my labour. I enjoy tidiness and seeing how much space I have gained. Suddenly, special pieces stand out as they are not hidden by the mess. I also get the satisfaction of being able to give a full bag of unwanted items to the charity shop.

Inner Space

Clutter makes you feel that your closet is too small even when it is a large one. Disorder has the tendency of taking up space. Unfolded clothes take more room than folded ones.

We all notice this phenomenon when we pack for our holidays. One minute, our suitcase is full to the brim of unfolded clothes and can't be zipped up. The next, our suitcase is half empty after we took a few minutes of time and care to fold and pack properly.

Once you have purged and tidied and sorted, space will open up for you in your closet. When you bring home a new garment, you will have room to introduce it in its proper place. No more cramming it in amongst the others to get unfolded, creased and unloved. No more pushing, pulling and shoving.

Positive Energy

When space is too cluttered, energy does not flow freely. Unused and unloved objects have a stale energy. To draw positive energy into your life, remove the clutter and replace it with beautiful and useable things that you love. Once you declutter, your home, relationships and even you will feel so much better because positive energy is allowed to circulate.

Discovery

One of the great positives about a good clear out is we find things which were long forgotten.

I am pretty sure I am not the only one who has chanced upon an old favourite that the decluttering has revealed. It lay long forgotten in a dark recess of the closet or was stuck over the back end of a drawer. An old favourite is much better than a brand new piece that has just been bought, don't you think? Old memories come flooding back and we start making new plans on how to wear it again. This discovery is enough to make our hard work pay off in one fell swoop. Now that's what I call success. What will you discover?

Better Dressed

As I mentioned earlier, with an untidy closet you don't have a clue what clothes are lurking in there. Some clothes fit you, some don't, some are so you, some definitely are not. But, because you tend to pick your clothes from the top of the pile or the front of the drawer, you end up wearing the same things over and over. There is nothing wrong per se, if these suit and fit you. But, it can a bit hit and miss. On most days, I'll wager it is more miss than hit.

Know that once you have cleared out the wrong stuff, you will be left with the right stuff. You will look 'soignée' and chic. You deserve better than 'that will do'.

Your motivation should now be beginning to sprout shoots. Let's give it some further TLC and see if we can get it to full flower.

CHAPTER 5

GET MOTIVATED!

"Our greatest weakness lies in giving up. The most certain way to succeed is always to try just one more time" - Thomas A. Edison

Active Versus Passive

One of the main reasons you are reading this book may be because you cannot make a commitment to clear out and tidy up. You may routinely use the same words for not tackling your clutter, such as 'try', 'hope', 'think' and 'wish'.

Your favourite sayings may be:

- I have tried to tackle this so many times...
- I have to try to find the time...
- I try every weekend...
- I have to try harder to do this next time...
- Believe me, I have tried...
- I have been hoping to do it for ages...
- Let's hope I can do this, next week...
- I hope I don't get distracted...
- I hope I can do the whole thing in one go this time...
- I have been thinking about it for weeks...
- When I think about it...
- I try not to think about it...
- I think I'll try harder next time...

- I wish I could get this tidied up...

- I wish I had more time...

- I wish I had a book to help me!

I could go on and on. Just as there is a 'me' in messy, remember there is an 'I' in tidy. It's up to you.

The words 'try', 'hope', 'think' and 'wish' are not action verbs. They are more like wishful thinking. When people use these words, they do not commit. To try is not to do. By saying "I shall try," they already give themselves the excuse that they may start but probably won't finish. Then, they give themselves an imaginary pat on the back with: "Well at least I tried." By trying, they plan and expect to fail.

The same can be said with the words 'hope' and 'think'. In other contexts, these words are appropriate. However, in this instance, they are not the right words to use.

Hoping to do something or thinking that you will do it one day, is not convincing yourself that you will actually do it.

The same goes for 'wish'. You don't sound serious enough and committed enough to do it.

The right words to use are 'do', 'now' and 'commit'. Replace the above with:

- Let's do it now!

- I am doing it!

- I am starting today!

- I am committed to doing it!

  Yes, I am willing myself to do it now!

Notice the whole difference, even in the tenses used. Instead of the past and future, these sentences are in the present. No more "I have tried" and "I hope that I shall," No more "if onlys" and wishful thinking. So far, these have not worked in your favour one iota, have they? If they had, you would not need any help now.

From now on, use action verbs and the present tense and energy. Notice the difference in tone and enthusiasm when you say "I am doing!" and "I am committed!" The exclamation marks show your enthusiasm for the task at hand. You now mean business and will not take no for an answer. This is more like it.

Allez, on y va!

Don't Dither, Do!

We are all so busy with our lives that we often choose the quickest route to benefit us immediately. Whilst this gives us the impression of helping at the time, it will not serve us in the long run. Taking shortcuts has a tendency to catch up with us and bite us on our proverbial derrière. Everything that we do has a knock-on effect. Let's see a few consequences of every day shortcuts, as they go from bad to worse:

Shortcut

We don't make time to tidy up as we go

Consequences

The mess mounts up

We have 'nothing to wear'

We think 'that will do'

We look frumpy

We don't look professional

We get passed over for promotion.

Shortcut

We leave our shoes where we take them off

Consequences

We can only find one

We spend ages looking for the other one

We are late into the shower

We miss the bus

We miss the date

We lose the guy.

Shortcut

We don't make time to look at our finances
and create a budget

Consequences

We don't stick to what we can afford

We spend more than we earn

Debts mount up

We have difficulty paying important bills

We may be declared bankrupt

We may lose our home.

It is always easy to be wise after the event. Doing what is necessary, and tackling jobs as they arise, is always preferable. When we don't do this, our alarm bells ring but we choose to ignore them for the short-lived lazy time it gives us. But, we soon feel guilty and stressed because things become worse. The solution is not to ignore your problems, or your alarm bells. Deal with things immediately. Meet things head on. So, don't dither. Do!

Visualise

As I mentioned earlier, we get overwhelmed by the sight of clutter. All we see is disorder and chaos. Just thinking about tidying up is a daunting task in itself. And that's before we even start to declutter. It is easy to lack motivation in these circumstances, especially when we have so many other things to do at home. So, how can you summon up any motivation for the job? I have found the following simple exercise extremely helpful.

- Try it now and see how you feel afterwards.

- Find a quiet place in your home away from the clutter you wish to clear.

- Sit down and close your eyes.

- Take slow, deep breaths, in through your nose and out through your mouth.

- Try to concentrate on your breathing only.

- Make yourself relax.

- Imagine walking into your bedroom. It is tidy, calm and, oh, so welcoming.

- Look around in your mind's eye. All you see are order and harmony.

- Enjoy looking around your beautiful, clean room.

- Feel how calm you have become.

- Go to your closet in your mind and feel yourself opening the doors slowly.

- What a beautiful sight lies inside!

- The contents of your closet are tidy, sorted and ordered.

- All your clothes are neatly hung and folded.

- Blouses, skirts, dresses and trousers

are sorted and grouped together.

- Your clothes smell fresh and clean.
- Everything is tidy and well looked after.
- Pass your fingers along the rail of neatly hung shirts and dresses.
- Feast your eyes on this haven of calm.
- Feel how relaxed and happy you are.
- Believe that it is possible to achieve this, as you have seen it.

When you choose to end this exercise, open your eyes. Feel how ready you are to replicate your room, as you saw it in your mind's eye. You are now happy to tackle the job. In fact, you just can't wait. I hope that you found this exercise fun and rewarding. Visualisation is a powerful tool that can help us to achieve our goals. When filled with uncertainty, taking the time to visualise the end result helps to remove doubts from our mind. The task becomes clearer. The steps that we have to take open up to us. Our goal then becomes achievable.

A Friend In Need

In order to motivate you even further, there are ways you can get your friends to help.

One way is to ask a good friend to come over and assist, either physically or emotionally. She can sort things with you or just sit on a comfy chair and spur you on. This is the soft option.

Be careful though not to let the occasion turn into a girls' afternoon in. Of course, you need to laugh and joke but you still have to finish the task today. Give yourselves a reward for later, such as a glass of wine and a movie.

Another idea is to choose a friend in the same situation as yourself and hold yourselves accountable to each other. Arrange to have a dedicated declutter day. You do this in your own homes but check up on each other during the day. You can Skype each other or you can send photos of your progress on your mobile. You are less likely to give up if you know that your friend is keeping to their side of the bargain. You won't wish to disappoint them.

The third option is for the really desperate. Those who, without a kick up the derrière, can't deal with the situation and so give up without trying.

The solution is to enlist the help of a declutter f(r)iend. You know the one, they are clean freaks and absolutely not the kind to let you off the hook easily. It is a hard decision to make, as you know that they will be in charge throughout the task. This may be the only way for you to complete it. Sometimes, you have to choose the hard way. No pain, no gain.

Sweet Reward

You've heard of the carrot and the stick. We can all do what we are told, when menaced with the stick. However, we get so much more enjoyment out of a job well done when promised a sweet little treat in return. That is what I recommend here. Think of something you would really enjoy. Treats can be all sorts of pleasant rewards.

- Here are a few ideas for you:
- Take a hot bubble bath while sipping a chilled glass of white wine
- Drink a refreshing fruit smoothie
- Bake a luscious cupcake (sorry I'm a foodie)
- Watch your favourite film
- Get a manicure or pedicure
- Receive a shoulder and back massage (from hubby?)
- Buy a new piece of jewellery

- Treat yourself to silk lingerie (you have to replenish your wardrobe, right?)
- Find time to sit down and read a good novel
- Relax!

Now we've got you motivated, let's do it!

CHAPTER 6

STEP BY STEP: LET'S DO IT!

"Three Rules of Work: Out of clutter find simplicity; From discord find harmony; In the middle of difficulty lies opportunity" – Albert Einstein

When you are overwhelmed by so much clutter, it is difficult to know which way to turn and where to start. You may worry how you could ever finish. I, too, get overwhelmed by a lot of mess and clutter. Just seeing it stresses me out and I can't think straight. I like my life and my home ordered. This is why I do my best not to let the clutter build up, but sometimes it just happens!

When I start tackling a big job like decluttering, I do not look at the whole room. On seeing the sheer scale of the situation, I might doubt whether I could handle it all by myself. Try to do the same thing today and not look at the room as a whole. You know the mess is there, believe me. Just be a robot for the next few minutes. Put your favourite dance music on. This will give you energy and lift your spirits. Think about something else for now. You will work faster, and you will finish in no time. However, if you look at the mess and focus on it before even starting, you may feel it is too much to cope with and lose hope.

Now you are ready to go, let's do it!

♥ Tip

Have plenty of water, a flask of coffee or tea at hand and maybe a snack or two. Turn your mobile off and put your answer-phone on. You could get side-tracked by something else (maybe this is what you want?) and stop this exercise in its tracks.

♥ Tip

If the weather allows, open the windows for fresh air to circulate around the room. This will oxygenate your body and give you more energy.

♥ Tip

Put your favourite music on. Choosing something lively, such as pop songs, will energise you and make you work faster. You never know, you may get into a rhythm of putting items away.

One-two-in the box

One-two-fold away

One-two-to keep

♥ Tip

If you have a TV set in your bedroom, resist the urge to turn it on. You will get distracted and slow right down. I can imagine you stopping during interesting moments of whatever TV show is on. Ignore the square box for now. You can watch it later when the job is all done.

Step 1: Ready!

You have already made the first step.
You've realised the problem you have with your cluttered and disorganised closet. You have accepted it is your responsibility and bought this book. This means that you have taken your head out of the sand and acknowledged that you need help tackling your clutter. Well done. Let's move on to step two now.

Step 2: Steady!

You are in the process of taking the second step: Reading this book, getting motivated and raring to go. You can't wait to get started. You are fed up with your over-filled closet. Your wardrobe does not work for your lifestyle. Neither does it enhance your body shape nor emphasise your best features. It is time to do something radical about it, not just think or talk about it. Time for step three!

Step 3: Go!

The third step is to actually do it.

You are all psyched up, I hope. No turning back and running for safety. No ifs, no buts. So, take a deep breath and let's do this together! One, two, three, go!

Step 4: What Do You Need?

Gather everything you need into the room so that you don't have to stop to fetch things. This will only disrupt the process and could make you quit altogether. Believe me, I've been there.

What you will need:

Boxes and carrier bags

Laundry basket

Ironing basket

Cleaning products

Hoover, broom/brush/dustpan

Dust cloths

Drinking water

A snack or two

Music

Camera/camera phone

Anything else you think you might need.

Prepare enough boxes or carrier bags to contain all the clothes that you will throw away, give away, store or mend.

Next, put your boxes or carrier bags on the floor, next to the bed:

One for items to keep

One for stuff you will throw away

One for items to sell

One for the Charity shop/give away

One for things you will store

One for all items that need mending

One for things that belong in another room

Laundry basket

Ironing basket.

Next, put on your most basic and comfortable outfit, such as vest and shorts or undress to your bra and panties. You might wonder why. The idea is to try the clothes that may no longer fit or suit you, as you go. In this way, you can decide there and then what to do with them, if you don't remember what they look like on you.

♥ Tip

Before emptying your closet, take photos of the mess, from different angles: shoes only, clothes only, close-up of an especially untidy pile and the whole closet. You can pin them on the inside of your closet doors later to remind you of what it was like before you decluttered. Or, you can choose to keep them as part of a vision board of before and after. It will make you feel good to see how far you have come, once it's all done.

Step 5: Skeletons In Your Closet

My experience has shown me that, if we tackle only one section of the closet or a few drawers at a time, we may be tempted to lose momentum and give up. However, emptying the whole closet and every drawer at once gives us the incentive to finish the task today.

So, with this in mind, empty the whole contents of your closet and drawers, pick up everything from the floor and put it all on top of your bed. Yes, everything. The reason is simple. Some of you may be tempted to delay the process and stop halfway through. The problem with stopping is that you may not complete the task. If you were to put everything on the floor, it would be easier to sidestep the mess and leave it there, maybe for days. I am pretty sure that some of you are now nodding in agreement. However, if you put it all on your bed, as you have to go to bed tonight, you have to complete the task.

I know some of you will think that I'm being tough on you but the softly-softly approach has not worked for you up to now, has it! You tried the 'one drawer at a time' strategy. You have used all sorts of excuses and look at the results:

your closet is still a mess.

Today is the day to sort this out. Think about how happy you're going to be later on.

So, let's go. Let's do this thing! Everything out!

When I say remove everything from your closet, I mean every, single thing. Do not be tempted to leave bits and bobs that don't belong there. I used to fool myself into thinking that I had decluttered my whole closet, knowing full well that various things never left it.

Objects such as an old postcard, an empty wallet or various trinkets, like little skeletons, remained entombed inside. I was not ready to get rid of them or didn't know where else to put them. Sometimes they stayed there, because I couldn't be bothered to find a place for them. I didn't use them, didn't love them, so why on earth did I keep them? My closet was never fully decluttered until the day I'd had enough and took everything out. Once these items were in the open air, I had to make a final decision there and then. So the postcard was thrown away and the others items were placed in the charity box. I hoped that somebody somewhere would cherish them more than I did. I felt liberated, as if a weight, albeit small, had been lifted.

Step 6: Clean

Now that the closet is completely empty, clean it inside and out. This is going to be the repository of your most fabulous clothes, the treasure chest of your most valued possessions. It deserves to be loved and taken care of.

A vacuum cleaner and a damp cloth do a good job of picking up the dust. You can also use a bucket of warm soapy water and a sponge, depending on how much cleaning there is to do. Remember to dry off any excess water thoroughly. Any way you choose to clean, you will be amazed at the amount of dust, dirt, sand and general grime that has gathered in there.

Start at the top and work down. Cleaning from top to bottom makes sense so that no dust falls onto your clean shelves. Pay particular attention to the top of the closet as this is where most of the dust gathers. Remove all the things that have managed to get up there, such as blankets, pillows, and other bits and pieces that you haven't previously removed. You will decide what you can do with these later.

Clean the inside well, getting into all the corners with your cloth or sponge.

Ensure the hanging rail is clean too.

Remove any tatty pictures or photos tacked inside the doors.

Give a good clean to the doors and drawers, inside and out. If you can move the closet easily without doing yourself an injury, hoover the back to remove cobwebs. I would also hoover the bedroom floor at this point to pick up any dust and debris.

Inspect the entire closet for any space you may have missed. Small items could still be left, wedged in behind a drawer or at the back of a bottom shelf. Some little critters always manage to stay hidden.

Now you've finished cleaning, remove the vacuum cleaner or bucket and all your cleaning paraphernalia from the bedroom. Put them in the hallway, out of sight. Some of you may be tempted at this point to put these away where they belong, in the utility room, basement, garage or kitchen. Be careful, you may get distracted and not come back. If this is likely to happen to you, please leave them by the door. You can tidy them up later. You have heard the saying: "Stay on the path!"

♥ Tip

Notice how much space you now have. Look on the shelves and on the rails. Enjoy the smell of cleanliness and the sight of space. Pat yourself on the back: job well done. Doesn't it make you feel good? Does it relax you? It does. Is it calming? Of course, it is. Try to visualise all your clothes neatly arranged on the shelves and on the hanging rail. Think of neat rows of shoes too. Aaah, bliss. You can take a photo at this stage, if you wish, either for yourself or for your declutter buddy.

♥ Tip

Take a photo of the mountain of stuff piled high on your bed. Ask yourself whether you need it all. Notice how nothing looks attractive or inviting. This will spur you on to the next step.

Step 7: Decision Time

Now is the time to go through your items one by one, making a decision as you go.

Should you keep, sell, give away, ditch or store? If in doubt, try things on. This is when you will find it practical to be in your underwear.

Ask yourself these questions before making a decision:

Does it fit me?

Does it suit my personality and my style?

Is it 'me'?

Does it make me say 'wow'?

Is it classic and good quality enough for multiple wears and/or years?

Will it go with as many of my other clothes as possible?

Is it too old, in bad condition or past its 'wear-by-date'?

Do I already have something similar?

Last but not least, does your hubby think you are sexy in it?

This step is the perfect opportunity to sort

your wardrobe and style out. Be critical when trying on your clothes before reaching any decision. If your reaction when you look at yourself in the mirror is 'wow', keep the item.

However, if it's anything less than that, such as 'oh dear', or even 'hahaha', then it has to go. This is the opportunity you have been waiting for. It is the chance to change your current style to a new, classier, you. Tell yourself that you are worth much more than a 'that will do'. Nothing less for you now than an 'oh là là!'

♥ Tip

Depending on the amount you have to sift through and how long you dither on each item, this process may take from an hour up to half a day. Keep in mind though, that the longer you take on this task, the more time you have to persuade yourself to keep more and throw away less.

♥ Tip

Put a timer on so that you are aware of the time you are spending. Give yourself a predetermined half hour or hour before you start. You can also use the length of your favourite CD. Otherwise you may never finish.

Step 8: Sorting

Now is the time to be putting things into the relevant boxes as you go.

Fill up your boxes or bags as follows:

To keep:

Classic pieces that are timeless

Good quality pieces

Clothes that fit your size and shape

Clothes in colours that suit your complexion

Clothes that you love

Clothes that make you and everybody else say 'wow' when you wear them.

Bear in mind the following little caveat. Just because you wear some clothes all the time does not mean that you should keep them. They could be the wrong style, shape, colour or fit for you. Be critical of every piece you keep. The clothes you choose to keep should fit as many of the above criteria as possible. Put them on. Take a good look in the mirror. Laugh or cry. I sure have on occasions. Then decide: is it a keeper?

The best way to reach a quick decision is to ask yourself: Do I look and feel fabulous in this? Yes or no? If you look great, keep it. If not, ditch it. No ifs, no buts.

♥ Tip

Tempted to keep too many things? Put the 'To Keep' box furthest away from you. As it will be more of an effort for you to stretch out to put things in there, this will act as a deterrent to keeping too much. The two boxes that should be closest to you are, you guessed it, the 'Throw Away' and the 'Charity' ones. Tadaa!

♥ Tip

Think of a Hollywood star or your favourite style icon. Imagine them making these decisions.

What would they give away, what would they keep? If some pieces would not be kept by them, why should you? Raise your standards.

Throw away:

Any item that is damaged and cannot be mended

Any piece that cannot be given away for any reason

Shoes with broken heels or too damaged

Any panties that have lost their elasticity or have gone grey

Bras that no longer hold anything up.

To sell:

Any items that are good quality can be turned into cash via any auction site. So sell pieces that are:

Good quality but no longer suit or fit you

That you no longer like.

Give away/charity box:

Fill this box with anything that is:

Low quality but in good condition and clean

Does not fit your current size (even if you plan to lose a few pounds; when you do, treat yourself to something new).

Too trendy (will look ridiculous in a month's time)

Does not suit your style or lifestyle (office wear if you now work in a garden centre, coats if you have moved to the tropics)

In a colour that does not suit your complexion

Out of fashion but not classic

Unworn for two years. I could have said one year but two years give you a more realistic timescale. On your next purge, you can then give away things you have not worn for one year.

Too loose and square shaped

Too mumsy

Too tight

And finally, those ghastly leggings.

♥ Tip

Don't keep dipping into the charity box to retrieve pieces that you think you want to keep after all. If you start doing this with one item, you will do it for more until the box is empty again. You cannot keep everything. I say to you: "Giving will set you free!"

♥ Tip

Feel good when putting each article into the

charity box. Think of the good you are doing. Feel good about giving. Needy people will benefit from the clothes. Charities will benefit from making extra revenue. You will have gained extra space. It is a win-win-win situation for all. Smile!

Storage:

Not of the current season (coats/jackets/woolly jumpers/boots if your decluttering is done during the summer; bikinis/strappy dresses/sun hats/flip-flops if it's currently winter)

For special occasions only (you only wear these once or twice a year, so no need to clutter your closet all year round)

Wedding dress/bridesmaid dresses/ball-gowns

Only store clean pieces

Store these under the bed, in your loft space, spare room, basement, or wherever is relevant for your home. If space is scarce, think about giving away or selling your old prom and bridesmaid dresses and all the other clothes you wore once and will never wear again. You don't have to keep everything.

Resist the temptation to pay for extra storage away from your home. This may only encourage you to keep non essential items somewhere else. Off-site storage is not the equivalent of decluttering, it is just moving stuff from one place to another, while still keeping everything.

♥ Tip

Some items for storage could in fact be items to sell or give away. Take photos as a keepsake or cut out a swatch of the fabric or detailing from an inconspicuous place, to treasure if you wish. If you have gone through a divorce, you may choose to sell or give away your wedding dress, especially if it brings back sad memories. You may feel just as nostalgic looking at a photo and it will not take as much space.

Mending:

There will be clothes, shoes and accessories that will need mending in some way. Fill this box with what you want to keep but which needs mending, such as buttons to sew on, hems to take up, heels and soles to replace. I don't go to the trouble for low quality pieces. I only get good quality ones mended. There is no need to throw good money after bad.

Laundry:

There are bound to be clothes that are dirty and dusty, if they have not been carefully kept. It is common sense not to put back into your closet any clothes that are not clean. Similarly, it goes without saying that there is no need to launder clothes that you intend to ditch.

Ironing:

Anything that is clean but needs ironing should go in here. If your closet was in a particularly bad state, you will find that plenty of your clothes need ironing or even washing. The extra work of having to iron clothes for a second time will be a lesson well learned.

Congratulations. You are almost there.

♥ Tip

Ask the kids to help you fill up the boxes

and put clothes in the appropriate piles. Children will absolutely love to help and will tell you off if you try to cheat by retrieving things.

They will also be honest enough to tell you in no uncertain terms, with glee even, which clothes they like on you and which they don't.

Children are great levellers when it comes to our egos!

♥ Tip

Try not to be tempted to create an extra pile of 'Don't Knows'. Trust me, if you don't yet know, these pieces are not likely to be 'wow' items. So, if your clothes are more a 'je ne sais pas' than a 'je ne sais quoi', give them away. You will have forgotten about them by tonight, I promise you.

Step 9: Double-Check

You are almost done. You went through all your clothes and distributed them between the various boxes and baskets. Take a little breather, you've earned it, ma chère.

This may sound quite harsh but, in a couple of minutes, make yourself go through every item in your 'To Keep' box. Be extra thorough this time. You may find that some 'Don't Knows' and 'Maybes' have crept in 'unnoticed', cough, cough.

It is simple really: If you don't know, don't keep! The 'mmm, that will do for my days off' need to be sent away. Remember to keep only things that make you go 'wow' when you wear them. Why should you look less than fabulous every day?

Step 10: Remove Temptation

At this point, it is a good idea to remove temptation by taking out all but the 'To Keep' box from your bedroom. You may feel the urge to reclaim items you had decided not to keep. So, take the 'Throw Away' box to the bin. The 'Sell' box can be put next to your computer, ready to list the items on your favourite auction site. Put the 'Charity' and 'Mending' boxes into the boot of your car or by the front door. And finally, take the 'Laundry' and 'Ironing' baskets to the utility room. All of this will ensure that you are only left with your 'To Keep' pieces.

♥ Tip

If you are still tempted to retrieve various pieces from your 'Charity' box, seal the box or bag with some wide packaging tape. Once sealed, you won't be likely to open it up.

Step 11: Divide And Conquer

That's it. You are only left with the 'To Keep' box. This step is about dividing and categorising the clothes that you are keeping. Do this by garment type before putting back into your closet.

Empty your 'To Keep' box onto your bed.

Make piles of:

Tops and T-shirts

Shirts and blouses

Sweaters and cardigans

Skirts

Trousers

Jeans

Dresses

Jackets and coats

Lingerie

Nightwear

Socks and tights

Belts, scarves, hats, gloves

Shoes and boots

Handbags.

Once all these are sorted, it is easier to see what you are left with. You will have more of an idea about where things will go.

In the next chapter, we shall look at different storage ideas. The subsequent chapter will help you organise your clothes in your closet.

CHAPTER 7

ORGANISATION AND STORAGE IDEAS

"Practical storage pieces are great if you have a basement or a garage. But when you actually live with them day in and day out, they should be beautiful to look at." - Thom Filicia

In the previous chapter, I showed you how to declutter. We are now moving on to organisation. A good system is worth its weight in gold. With your clothes and accessories well arranged, you will gain time, dress better and, last but not least, regain your sanity.

In this chapter, we look at storage ideas that you can use to organise your clothes in an efficient and aesthetic way. Finding what works best for you may be a matter of individual choice but for any system to work, it must correspond with the way you live. Let's read on.

Some Closets Are More Equal Than Others

For various reasons, the size and style of women's closets vary. Many have a closet and a chest of drawers, others may be lucky enough to have their own walk-in closet. The latter is a dream for most women, me included. Yet others, where every inch counts, have to make do with a few drawers and a small hanging rail. So the question is, how can you store all your clothes so that your closet looks inviting and is, above all, functional? There is such a natural beauty in form married with function, let's use it.

The primary task is to declutter and remove all your unused and unwearable clothes. You should have already done this in the previous chapter. The more useful stuff you keep, the better your wardrobe will look and serve you.

If your budget allows, most closet retailers provide a design service tailored to your needs. They will bring your closet into the 21st century. For those of you who cannot afford this service, I shall give you a few simple storage ideas. These are by no means exhaustive. There are plenty more out there. Just find what works best for you.

Hanging Rail

A hanging rail is a hanging rail. Well, yes. But some work better for you than others.

There are two types of closet rails: The one that runs left to right and the one that runs front to back.

With the first, you can see all your clothes from the side. It is easy to find the piece you want.

The second type only allows you the sight of the first piece, albeit in full view. The items hung behind the first will not likely see the light of day. You will tend to grab the clothes that hang at the front, because it is easier than struggling to pull out what is behind. For this reason, I prefer the left-to-right rails.

Hangers

Most people have a mix of wire, plastic and wooden hangers, of different shapes and sizes. Wire and plastic hangers give your clothes unsightly sharp creases, especially with woollens. They render your clothes unwearable unless you wash and iron them again. Who has the time for this?

Personally, I love wooden hangers. They are more expensive than plastic or wire ones but your clothes will not have those unsightly marks on the shoulders.

Wooden hangers are not so expensive that you can't afford them. You don't have to replace all your wire hangers straight away. Replace them a few at a time, when you can. Put them on your shopping list to remind you to keep a look out for them.

To ensure that wooden hangers give the rail a more uniform look, buy them in bulk from the same retailer.

Paint the inside of your closet white or another pale neutral. Next, paint your wooden hangers to match. Your clothes will then take centre stage. Avoid using a bright colour, as it will give a colour cast to your clothes, especially your whites. A dark colour, meanwhile, would make the inside of your closet look like a dungeon. Not the look you are after, unless you are into '50 shelves of grey'.

Multi-Hangers

To save on space, buy multi-hangers. They are very handy to have. You can hang a number of skirts or trousers, cascading from the same hook. All or most of your skirts and trousers will be hung in one place. This will save you time instead of flipping through hangers.

Shelves

Shelves are the most popular storage choice, due to their versatility. Whether deep or narrow, widely spaced or close together, they offer so many ways to stack and show off your most prized possessions. You can display your collection of shoes or vintage handbags, T-shirts or jeans. Attractive storage trays or boxes can hold multiple items in one place on open shelves, while keeping the look tidy and uniform. It is up to you to make shelves attractive by using the power of your imagination.

♥ Tip

Line the walls of your closet with adjustable shelves, wall to wall. By moving them around, you can change the look and use of these whenever you feel like it.

♥ Tip

If the idea of plain colour in your closet does not appeal, let your creativity run wild.

Paint polka dots, stripes, hearts or any design you fancy on your shelves.

Cover them with funky wallpaper.

Add edging fabric along the front.

Tack or glue fancy buttons, sequins or bows along the edge.

Don't forget to send me photos :0) I would love to see your ideas.

Matching Boxes

It is all very well storing things in boxes. If you want harmony, choose boxes of the same colour, shape or style. This will help you to maintain an overall tidy and neat closet. If the boxes are mismatched, your shelves will look busy.

If you are a fan of shabby chic, you may find vintage boxes in charity shops or online. If you are a retro 'freakette', antique shops or flea markets may be good hunting grounds. It is entirely up to you. Let your individuality shine.

Storage Concepts

The following storage concepts may give you ideas for your own closet.

Using acrylic trays or cutlery trays to showcase and separate your jewellery is better than having them all jumbled up together.

Alternatively for necklace and bracelets, you can use a cork board and hang them on pins or hooks. You can hang earrings from the rims of pretty glass jars or crystal glasses.

Storage boxes can utilise dead space under

the bed. They will prevent you from throwing things under there, to be lost or forgotten. To avoid damp and mould, choose hermetically-sealed boxes in all cases or ensure that they are aired frequently.

Although I prefer to use uniform boxes, you may like to choose an eclectic collection of:

Lacquer boxes

Japanese bento boxes for small items

Vintage crates

Old trunks

Rolling carts

Stacking boxes

Cubes

Hat boxes

Vintage suitcases

Wooden buckets

Old toy boxes

Pretty & decorative storage boxes in various materials.

Clear shelves and containers allow you to see the contents at a glance, without having to open boxes all the time.

Do be careful, Perspex scratches and becomes opaque with heavy use.

If you are lucky to have a walk-in closet, you can display all your shoes on shelves instead of on the floor. This removes the clutter and gives your shoes centre stage.

Hang your handbags from shower curtain hooks in the closet or on a separate rail, instead of leaving them on the floor. For this purpose, metal hooks will look better than plastic. You can decorate the hooks with fabric, ribbons or paint.

A hanging shoe organiser may not look pretty but it saves space on the floor. It also prevents your shoes getting damaged. As I have never seen any pretty ones, why not create your own? They are so simple in design, that anyone handy with a sewing machine, could create one out of their favourite fabric.

Don't be afraid to use all available vertical space, even up to the ceiling, to give you maximum storage choice.

Do be careful when using high shelves. Have an appropriate and safe method of reaching them, such as an old set of library steps, or a long-handled reacher/grabber.

♥ Tip

Before throwing away containers, boxes or anything that may be helpful, try to brainstorm how you could recycle them in your house.

Sometimes, the most mundane of household items can be used in a most unconventional way that frees up space or provides an imaginative way to store things. You never know, you could become the new queen of organisation.

Shoe Boxes

Storing shoes in plastic transparent boxes allows you to see them at a glance and protects them from scratches and dust.

Shoe racks make your closet look organised but take considerable space on the floor. Alternatively, have those shoe racks fixed to the wall.

♥ Tip

Some new shoes come with fabric bags. Use them when travelling to keep your shoes or dirty laundry in. Or use them as organisers in your suitcase.

♥ Tip

Instead of costly drawer liners, simply dab a couple of drops of your favourite perfume, eau de toilette or essential oil on a piece of cotton wool. Place it at the back of your drawers or shelves. The fragrance will permeate the clothes, keeping them fresh and sweet smelling. Ensure the oil does not come into contact with any fabric, as it could stain.

From storage ideas, we now move on to organising your wardrobe. This is the final stage in transforming your closet from clutter zone to oasis of calm.

CHAPTER 8

ORGANISING YOUR WARDROBE

"Simplify, simplify" - Henry David Thoreau

You have rid yourself of your surplus clothes and accessories and sorted what is left into categories. Now let's see what we can do about arranging them back into your closet. I shall give you ideas on how to fold and hang each category of garment. Nothing here is rocket science, but for some of you, this may be something you are unaware of. So let's carry on. We want this decluttering task finished as soon as possible, don't we, ladies? Let the fun begin.

The first thing to do is to look at your closet and analyse your available space.

Ask yourself the following questions:

How many drawers do I have?

How wide and deep are my shelves?

How long is my hanging rail?

How much floor space is there?

Once you have answered the above, you can decide where every garment and accessory will fit. The amount of stuff and the available space determine where and how you put it all back in.

Organisation

I recommend three tried and tested ways to organise your clothes:

1. By garment type:

Lingerie

Sleepwear

Tops

Shirts

Sweaters

Skirts

Trousers

Dresses

Jackets

Coats

Socks/tights/stockings

Hats/gloves/scarves

Shoes

Boots

Handbags

When sorted in groups such as these, it is easy to find the clothes you need and the arrangement is more aesthetically pleasing to the eye. The above list will vary according to what you decide to fold and keep on shelves or to hang on a rail. I like to fold my T-shirts and some of my tops and sweaters. I also fold my jeans. I hang my shirts, blouses and cardigans.

2. By colour

Organising by colour, from light to dark, on a rail or on a shelf makes for a visually well ordered closet. Whether it is from left to right on a rail or top to bottom on the shelves is up to you. This way you can go directly to the colour you need, no searching.

3. The Combination

For an even better result, you can combine the above two methods: By garment type and then by colour.

This makes sense. When you need a dress, you go straight to your dress section and then choose the colour you want. This is my favourite arrangement. Otherwise, it is still a bit too higgledy-piggledy for me.

Now you have decided where things are going to, how are they going to be displayed in the closet? Will they be folded or hung? Let's look at each garment type in turn.

Tops And T-Shirts

I fold my tops and T-shirts the following way. I first decide how wide my stack of tops needs to be (taking into account that tops may have different collar widths). I then lie the top to be folded flat, front down, with its collar to the left and bottom edge to the right. I then neatly bring each side edge over towards the centre, giving me the appropriate width. I then fold the sleeves, so that the outside edge of the sleeve is either parallel to the side edge of the garment (if they are long) or parallel to the shoulder line (if they are short). I finish by folding the bottom edge towards the collar. Et voilà, a neatly folded T-shirt.

Once folded, they are stacked neatly on the shelves.

Sort them further by colour. I prefer to stack with light colours at the top and darker ones at the bottom of the pile. But, you might prefer to do the opposite, as long as it works for you.

If you have plenty of tops and enough room to do this, two lower stacks, instead of a high one, will prevent them falling over.

♥ Tip

Light colours show creases more than darker ones. So, put white and lighter colours at the top of the stack, which will crease them less than if the garments are at the bottom.

Shirts

Shirts ought to be hung on their own hangers, one on each.

As we saw previously, avoid using wire hangers for your shirts. They will leave nasty creases on the shoulders. Use wider wooden ones instead.

Do not put more than one shirt on any one hanger. They would become too creased, especially on the collars, shoulders and front panels.

Button shirts all the way up, so they keep their shape better. To save time, you may decide that two buttons are enough. If so, button the top one and one half-way down.

You should not hang shirts too tightly together or the collar will lose its shape and crease.

Sort them by colour, white to black.

A freshly ironed and hung group of shirts is a joy to behold.

Sweaters

Sweaters can be stacked on a shelf. Ensure that you fold them with care as some folds can give unsightly creases.

Alternatively, put them on a wooden or padded hanger.

Do not use plastic or wire hangers as they are particularly nasty to wool.

Little Cardigans

My preference is to hang cardigans on a wooden hanger, fastening three buttons, top, middle and bottom. As little cardigans can look dressier than a sweater, this ensures that they are crease-free and ready to be worn.

Skirts

Hang your skirts on skirt hangers, light to dark. You can hang them by the waist or by the small ribbon loops attached to the inside of the garment. A word to the wise however is that hanging A-line skirts from the loops does not work too well. This is because their weight and shape causes the upper part of the skirt to sag and the sides to crease. Therefore, unless your skirts are straight cut, such as pencil skirts, hang them by the waist. Your ironing basket will thank you later.

With multi-hangers as mentioned above, you can hang four to six skirts, one below the other on the same hanger, if space is at a premium. An added advantage of this space saving idea is that these skirts are hung all together and in an ordered way.

♥ Tip

If your skirts are made of thin fabric, skirt hanger clips may leave marks on the waistline. You can avoid this by placing a dry makeup remover pad under each clip, to act as a cushion. Hey presto, no more marks.

Dresses

Hang your dresses on hangers, zipped up and buttoned to keep their shape and avoid creases. You can hang the loops attached to the garment on the hanger too. This ensures that the dress does not slide off the hanger, especially so for evening dresses.

If the dress is part of a suit, hanging the jacket over it makes for a quick retrieval in the mornings.

Outfit-To-Go

Another simple way to hang your clothes is by outfit. This is especially practical if you need five days' worth of office clothes.

Here are a few ideas for such 'prêt-à-porter' outfits for each day:

Monday

Dress - jacket - belt - jewellery

Tuesday

Top - skirt - cardigan - jewellery

Wednesday

Shirt - trousers - jacket - belt - jewellery

Thursday

Blouse - suit (skirt + jacket) - belt - jewellery

And for dress-down Friday

Top - jeans - belt - jewellery

In addition, for a complete 'outfit-to-go', wrap a pair of tights/stockings and underwear around the top of each hanger and place shoes under the ensemble. If you only have one or two pairs of work shoes, leave them by the front door. In the morning, all you have to do is pull out a whole outfit in one go. As these outfits are all ready to wear, you can't get more 'prêt-à-porter' than this!

Jeans

There is no need to hang jeans, especially when space on the rail is at a premium. They are fine when folded. Jeans do not crease like other trousers, as denim is so durable. The only time they get creased is fresh out of the washing machine. I used to keep seven pairs of jeans, all clogging space. I went through them one day. I discovered two pairs I only wore for walking the dogs, one short length to wear with flats, one boot cut, one skinny and two I never wore at all. The last two I gave away. If I never wore them, what was the point of keeping them? The ones for walking the dogs I put, along with my trainers and jacket, in my coat cupboard, by the front door. I was then left with the three I wore regularly: short, boot cut and skinny. They are all I needed. How many do you need?

♥ Tip

2 ways to fold jeans

Lay jeans flat. Fold one leg over the other so that the legs are on top of each other.

You then have two choices:

1/ Fold them in thirds. This is good if your shelves are not too high but your jeans will take more space lengthwise.

2/ Or in quarters. These will be shorter but take more space in height.

Whatever you do, do not fold jeans with a crease down the front of the leg. That is much too 70s.

♥ Tip

No need to throw away a pair of bootleg jeans if you now only wear straight-legged cuts.

Have them taken in by your seamstress. I have seen it done and you cannot tell the difference. You'd think they are original straight legged.

Trousers

Suit trousers should be hung from the waist, in their natural pleats. From personal experience, smart trousers will crease at the knees when folded over the bar of trouser hangers. This is why I keep mine hung from the waistline.

♥ Tip

Use foam-covered hangers for folded trousers to avoid any unsightly creases.

Suits

Suit pieces should be kept together on the same hanger. If you hang them up as soon as you take them off, the warmth of your body will assist the creases to fall out, helping to maintain that well pressed look. Keep them aired overnight, before hanging back in the closet.

Lingerie

You can store your underwear in a drawer, folded up in little stacks, sorted by colour and/or type. Some people prefer to store them by sets, bra and knickers together.

Only keep the bras that actually fit you now. Get your bust measured during your next lingerie shopping trip. Remember that bras that are past their 'wear-by-date' will not create uplift but rather the opposite.

By wearing badly fitting bras, your bust will sag and add inches to your silhouette. Please remove any bras not up to the job from your collection. Take it from a French woman, your love life will be the happier for it!

Jackets And Coats

Thick and bulky items such as jackets and coats can be hung on one side of the closet or in a separate coat cupboard. Of course, when not in season, they should be put away in storage. Having a dedicated coat cupboard will save space in your closet. On another practical note, hanging the coat next to the front door when you come in enables you to put away your bulkiest item as soon as you arrive. You don't have to carry your coat through the house to your bedroom, especially if it's wet. It is also ready to go by the front door when you next go out.

♥ Tip

Try to avoid hanging a jacket or coat on a hook by the little ribbon at the neck. This will distort the fabric. Always put them on a hanger, if possible.

♥ Tip

Empty pockets of jackets and coats before putting them away in the closet. You may have crumpled tissues, receipts, ticket stubs, coins or even a winning lottery ticket in there. Do the same with the contents of your handbag. Clutter finds its way into everywhere and into everything. The next time you use them, they will feel fresher and more cared for.

Sleepwear

Nighties, pyjamas and nightgowns can be folded and kept on a shelf in your closet or in a drawer. Silk nighties can be hung on padded hangers to keep them crease-free. You might choose to store more special pieces in pretty storage boxes, as befit their status.

Accessories

Belts can be hung on their own hangers. Alternatively, you can keep them on the same hanger as the skirts and trousers with which you wear them. Yet another way is to roll them up and put them in a storage box.

I prefer to keep my hats, gloves and scarves in boxes. They are difficult to keep neatly on a shelf. They have a tendency to slip and slide off.

If you keep all your gloves in the same box, the likelihood of losing one of a pair is low. Another way is to keep pairs together by forming a glove ball.

Single Sock Sadness Syndrome: heard of it? Let me explain. It is keeping our single socks in the sock drawer hoping their partner will resurface one day. Let me tell you one thing: they won't. If, after all your washing and ironing have been done, and they have not resurfaced, ditch the singletons. Or, use them as dusting gloves, or as glove puppets for the kids.

Handbags

I have found that handbags can be the most difficult items to store. Some lose their shape if not hung, some take up too much room, and we all seem to have too many to be able to store on one shelf only. Sometimes, you just want a whole wall dedicated to your handbags. Who wouldn't? Dream on!

Back in the real world, let's see what we can do with our little darlings.

You can hang them or keep them standing up on a (large!) shelf inside or outside your closet.

What about this storage idea? Fix a rod vertically to a wall, with hooks strategically placed along it. Hang your bags from the hooks. You can see and retrieve each one easily. No more rummaging through your bags to find the one you are looking for.

♥ Tip

When storing leather handbags for a while, fill them with crumpled paper. This will help them to keep their shape and prevent unsightly creases from forming. It will also minimise damp.

♥ Tip

Try not to place your handbag on the floor in public places or on public transport. It will collect all sorts of nasty stuff on the underside. If you were then to put it on your lap, you would get dirty marks. Ewwwww! Keep your handbag on your lap or at your side at all times.

♥ Tip

Empty and clean the inside of your handbags regularly. Handbags can and do harbour plenty of clutter, germs and dirt. Just like your closet, your handbag needs a declutter now and then.

Shoes

Most of us can say that we have too many shoes, but none of us ever will.

Even after storing my 'out of season' pairs, my 'in season' shoes were still piled two to three pairs high on the floor of my closet.

My 'out of season' shoes were piled six or seven high in boxes in my spare room! One afternoon, I finally went through them all and gave away twelve pairs in one go. I felt such a relief. It was my first ever purge. Since then, I go through my shoes regularly and get rid of one or two pairs, each time. I have also drastically reduced the amount I buy. My days of buying indiscriminately are well over. I am older and so much wiser. What about you?

There are many ways to organise shoes: on shoe racks, in boxes, on shelves or sitting at the bottom of your closet. I keep mine in a variety of ways, depending on which season it is.

When out of season, my shoes are stored in a shoe rack in a spare room. Boots are stored away in their own box when not in season, with cardboard, a shoe tree or rolled magazine inside, to keep their shape. I keep my expensive shoes, especially patent ones, wrapped in tissue paper or shoe bag, and in their original box. Keeping them in their original shoe box allows you to stack them and protect them.

When in season, my shoes are kept at the bottom of my closet, in their original boxes. Sneakers, ballet flats, sandals and ordinary every day shoes are put together, as a pair and standing up, in a chic, open basket, at the bottom of my closet.

♥ Tip

Try to keep on top of repairs.

Have your leather shoes resoled and re-heeled regularly.

Give them a good coat of polish too. They will only look better with age.

♥ Tip

Ensure shoes are ultra comfortable before buying or you will never want to wear them. They will clog your closet unnecessarily.

If shoes pinch at the toes or rub at the heel when you try them on, they will be painful to walk in. So, try using silicone foot pads to alleviate these problems. I do use them for a couple of pairs of mine.

Unfortunately, some shoes only start to get uncomfortable after being worn for an hour or two. This is something you cannot notice by just trying them on in the shop for a few minutes. If they are still uncomfortable, even with shoe pads, feel confident that you can't wear them at all and give them away without hesitation.

If they do not give you any pleasure, which is something shoes should do, why keep them?

♥ Tip

An extreme way to get rid of surplus shoes is to pretend that you are going away for a year.

Which shoes would you take away with you? Keep only those and give away the rest. Job done, the decision has been made for you. As I said, this is extreme.

Congratulations! Everything is now back in your closet, neatly organised and beautifully arranged. Give yourself a pat on the back or allow yourself your promised treat. Send a photo to your declutter friend.

In the next chapter, you will get advice on how to keep up the good work.

CHAPTER 9

KEEP UP THE GOOD WORK

"Less is more" - Christoph Martin Wieland

That's it. Decluttering and organisation are complete. Notice how good it makes you feel. A sense of achievement is washing over you right this minute. You've earned it. Well done. Let's see what you can do to keep on top of things from now on.

List

You now have the beginnings of a classic wardrobe. It is simple, versatile and, above all, wearable. Let's build on it.

So that you know where you're going, make a list of the few essential items that may be missing from your wardrobe. You don't have to do this today but try to have it ready for your next shopping expedition. Shopping without a list is like shopping blindfolded. You won't know which piece will be the one you need.

I have lists for everything and love ticking things off as I go. If you have a plan, you are less likely to buy on a whim. And as you know from bitter experience, if you buy one unsuitable piece, others will soon follow. This time next year, you will have to purge again.

So instead, go shopping armed with your list. Pace yourself. Shop around. Find out where the best clothes are. See if you can wait for the sales in order to get the best value, if you are strapped for cash at the time.

Sales

Try not to succumb to the buying frenzy in the sales. I never go on the first day because people go crazy and push you about. They grab just about anything when the price is reduced. It is too easy to make impulse purchases when we see other women buying. We think we may miss out on something and the shops rely on this. We have no time to stop and think. Refuse to follow the herd. Your purse and your wardrobe will thank you.

By avoiding the mad rush, you will be able to keep your wits about you and make an informed purchase. There will be shorter queues at the fitting rooms, which means less time spent at the shops.

Some people, on sales days, buy without trying things on. They then discover that the clothes they bought do not fit or suit them. Some don't return them so these clothes stay in their closet, unworn, with tags still on. It is all a big waste of money, time and space. This can also make us feel guilty as, every time we look at these clothes we bought, we wonder why we did it.

So please, make your life simpler, calmer and happier by shopping with a list, avoiding the rush and refusing to be pressured into making a decision you may later regret.

Awareness

Whilst on the subject of sales and shopping, why not try to find out the reasons behind your buying habits? It will be an interesting and useful exercise that will help you find out more about yourself. You may find that you buy mindlessly, following others without thinking, just like a robot. Or, maybe you find shopping a relaxing thing to do after a long day at work or on days off.

In any purchase there are two fundamental driving forces to consider. The need or desire to spend money (money driven) and the need or desire to have an object (object driven).

The two do not necessarily co-exist in any purchase.

Could it be that shopping fills a void in your life and that it helps you forget sad events? In this case it is the spending of money that you need to focus on. Or maybe you bring things into your life that you missed out on, as a child? Some older people who missed out in WWII, during their childhood, can go on filling their home with all sorts of things, whether toys or dolls, that they didn't have during the war. In this case, you must consider the actual items that you are buying more carefully.

If you generally buy without thinking, stopping and considering the whys of your purchase will be insightful. Whatever the reason, you may find the following exercise interesting to do.

Exercise:

Next time you feel like buying a non-essential item, do the following:

Firstly, ask yourself what is the driving force behind this purchase.

Is it the desire or need to spend money?

Or, is it your need or desire for the object?

If it is the object, ask yourself the following.

Why do you want it?

How does the thought of having it make you feel?

How will you feel about it after you have bought it?

How would you feel about leaving this piece in the store and not buying it right now?

Do you feel that you can go home and think about it?

If it is the thought of spending money, ask yourself the following.

Why do you want to spend money?

How does the thought of spending money make you feel?

How will you feel about it after you have spent money?

How would you feel about not spending money right now?

Do you feel that you can go home and think about it?

Whether your buying habit is object or money-driven, the answers may give you some clues about yourself that you had not considered before.

Do you just want 'stuff', in which case you may need to change your belief and attitudes about acquiring things.

Or, do you just have a need to spend money, in which case you may have deep seated issues about wealth and poverty that you need to address.

Once you know the reasons for your buying habits, you can ensure that you only buy things that you need and have a use for. You will also be less vulnerable to the psychological ploys that shops use to get you to part with your cash.

There is an old proverb that says "Know thyself." If you truly 'know yourself', your wardrobe will reflect the new empowered you. Great things will lie in store for you (no pun intended).

One In, One Out

Why not remove one item from your closet for every new item you bring in?

By replacing one item with a new one, it will help keep the amount of stuff in check. Space is limited. The replacing of items does no have to be like for like, but generally, will be.

If you do not wish to part with any item, due to sentimental reasons or good quality, even though you never wear it, put it in storage. As you create your new wardrobe, you may come across pieces you want to replace in the future. This could be because they either do not suit you, are of less quality or you would just prefer to update them. However, because of finances, you may have to hold on to them for the time being. So, as and when you can afford to replace them, adopt the one in, one out, rule.

When you bring a new garment in, immediately consign the old one to the bin or charity box.

The Iron, The Ditch And The Wardrobe

I used to keep, at the bottom of my ironing basket, a few pieces that I never ironed because they were awkward to iron or because I didn't like them much.

One day, I decided enough was enough. I put them in a carrier bag and took them to the charity shop. Not only did it give me more space in my ironing basket but I could actually have the satisfaction of seeing all my ironing done.

So, if you have pieces lingering at the bottom of your ironing basket that you never iron, ditch them and your wardrobe will be the better for it.

Appreciation

Appreciation seems like an idea from the distant past. The last few decades have seen a surge in our standard of living and spending power.

In addition to being able to spend more, there has been an increase in low priced goods in the High Street and in shopping malls. We have been able to satiate our primitive need to acquire. It may have something to do with keeping up with the Joneses and wanting to belong to the same in-crowd. It may simply be due to the fact that more choice is available, coupled with the ease of shopping and spending. As online stores keep your payment details, it has become easier and less time consuming to shop online. With a click of a button ("Buy Now With One-Click") you can use your credit card. Blink and you've spent it.

Decades ago, before credit became the norm, people had to scrimp, save and do without, in order to buy what they wanted. Now, we just 'put it on the card', or on the 'never never'. How many times have you paid by credit card in a shop and not even looked at the total amount? It is funny how the 'never never' has turned into the 'ever ever', with the APR stacking up.

I find that, with this ease of consumption, has come a disinterest and lack of appreciation of our purchases and of what we own. If we had to either pay cash or save for months for this pair of shoes, handbag or dress, wouldn't we buy less? Wouldn't we take more care of them and appreciate them?

Instead, we allow them to fall off hangers, get thrown in a heap at the bottom of the closet, or squashed in a drawer. We don't seem to care.

Maybe, while we are still in this seemingly endless recession, we should try to appreciate the things we buy and those we already own. This might make us curb our spending.

Once our closet is decluttered and tidy, we can start looking at every piece with a renewed interest. We made an active decision to keep these items. So, let's look at the quality of these clothes or accessories. Let's take the time to admire their beauty, detailing and great finish. Let's appreciate the natural fabric, great workmanship, and versatility. We can now see these pieces in a new light. Once we put them on, we can relish them even more. I have found that appreciation makes me happier and thankful that I can wear such a beautiful piece. Develop a habit of looking at your clothes in an interested manner. Feel how the fabric moves in your hands. Look at the finish and appreciate the work it has taken to create it. Mentally thank that person who made it. Try to find as many ways to wear that piece as you can. When you start appreciating and loving what you have, you will be less likely to buy blindly.

Use Your Best

As well as appreciating our things, we should use them more. Instead of waiting for Sundays, smart soirées or a day that never comes, let's wear them as often as we can. Instead of 'Sunday best', why not 'Tuesday best' or 'Thursday best'? Let's aim for 'every day best'. Make every day special enough to wear your best clothes and use your most precious accessories. This will make you feel extra special and chic. Why not look and feel great every day?

Tidy Up Every Day

Nothing puts you in a better mood than getting up in the morning and being surrounded with tidiness and order, instead of mess and chaos.

When you are in a happy mood, you are more likely to tidy up as you go.

So, do the following:

Hang your clothes when you take them off.

Put your dirty laundry in the basket instead of leaving it on the floor.

Place your jewellery back in its box.

Carefully lift the top of a stack of clothes when pulling out a top. Don't leave the stack in disarray.

Insert shoe trees inside your boots to keep them straight.

If you didn't do this when you went to bed, do it in the morning. If you leave it, it may become the slippery slope back to untidiness and mayhem. If you fail to do this step every day, soon the situation will become too overwhelming to deal with. You will procrastinate more and more until the mess becomes unbearable. Then you will have to do another big purge. In the meantime, you will have stressed out unnecessarily.

The state of your closet may well be a symptom of other problems in your life that you refuse to tackle as and when they arise. You let them build up until it is too late and you can no longer cope.

Whatever your reason or excuse, lack of time, fear of confrontation or just plain old laziness, try to break this cycle of negativity. Grab the bull by the horns and do what needs to be done. Straight away is always better than later. You will have less to do and it will be less stressful than letting things build up. You will have the added satisfaction of having done it. The truth is, things are never as bad as we imagine them to be.

Habit Or Behaviour

Studies have shown that successful people develop good habits. Some swear by the 21-day rule, others prefer 30 days. The premise is that, in order to develop an action into a habit, you practice it for 21 or 30 consecutive days. 'Consecutive' being the operative word. If you miss one or two days, you have to start again from the first day.

After this initial period, you will have formed a habit, but not yet a behaviour. For your habit to become a behaviour, you would have to do it for 90 consecutive days.

So, let's say you want to develop the habit of keeping your closet tidy. If you do this every single day for a month without fail, then you will have acquired the habit. Carry on for a further two months to ensure that it becomes part of your daily routine.

Our lives are filled with behaviour. Some people need to read before going to sleep, some require a strong cup of coffee on their way to work, others never miss the 6 O'clock news on TV. Other behaviours involve a sequence of actions, for instance when we first get up, we look at the time, go to the bathroom, have a shower, brush our teeth, get dressed and have breakfast. Are you in any doubt about the power of these habit forming rules? If so, consider that you had already formed a 30-day habit and 90-day behaviour of not tidying up! That behaviour is extremely difficult to break, isn't it?

Whether you call this a habit or behaviour, you do this without thinking about it. So let's use our ability to create habits and create some that benefit us and our lives. What about tidying up after ourselves, putting our dirty clothes in the laundry basket instead of on the floor, or do tasks as and when they arise? Soon clutter will be a thing of the past and your home will be a haven of tidiness. Ah, bliss.

♥ Tip

Keep a box or bag near your front door on a permanent basis for charity. Try to put in at least one item a day. It doesn't have to come from your closet only but from any room in the house as well. Little by little, your house will become less messy. Hopefully, by getting rid of things every day, even if only one item at a time, you will soon create a habit of giving. As a result, you will become more selective about what comes into your home.

Of course, now and again, you will go the whole hog and have a good clearing out. But in between, you can try to keep things in check and not let it develop into a full blown nightmare.

Purge Seasonally

When you form the habit of putting things away, huge purges, like the one you've just been through, will no longer be necessary. However, things get acquired during the year. If you have not gotten rid of one thing for every other that you brought in, you will need another purge, albeit a small one, now and again.

My favourite time to purge is at the beginning of spring and autumn. Multitasking, or at least double-tasking, is something I love doing. As I am going through my closet to declutter anyway, I kill two birds with one stone and swap over the seasonal pieces.

Spring/summer stuff in, autumn/winter stuff out, and vice-versa. I recommend going through the entire closet. If you've been keeping things tidy, go through your clothes by garment type. Keep those you will definitely wear next year and give away or sell those you won't. Keep things tidy or straighten things as you go.

You can also carry out a purge on the incoming season's clothes. You may have kept something thinking you will wear it, but now decide you won't. This will make you sift through your closet twice a year, keeping your closet under control. If you live in places where you do not have seasonal temperature differences, such as in the tropics, make yourself do this exercise twice a year anyway. Why not January, for the extra Christmas presents, and July for instance?

Holding On / Can't Let Go

If you are new to decluttering, you will discover that it is not only a physical process, but an emotional one too. There will be times when you won't be able to give some special pieces away. It will feel painful to even think of letting go of an old dress or pair of shoes, which you hold some sort of attachment to. It's normal to feel like this sometimes. Obviously, if you cannot bear to part with any of your stuff at all, then Houston we have a problem. I shall tell you what worked for me. On my very first purge, there were many items that I could not part with. So they stayed put. On my second purge, some went. And even more on my third. I found it less and less challenging to give clothes away the more often I challenged myself about why I was keeping them. It does become less painful each time, honestly.

Here are a few ideas for you to try:

During every decluttering, try hard to part with pieces that are no longer of any use to you. You may know this is the thing to do but still feel unable to part with them. If it is really that painful for you and stirs up many cherished memories, just keep that dress or that hat. You don't have to suffer and live with regret. Maybe next time, you will be able to. The right time will present itself. If there are items that are too special to let go, then rejoice in what they mean to you. Keep them, by all means. I am not advocating that you cannot keep things that you cherish. All I am saying is that, far too often, we hang on to things that we no longer truly cherish or that have no purpose in our lives.

If you decide to throw away an item but are still working towards doing so, why not keep it in sight in your bedroom? You could hang it up over the closet door or display it on your chest of drawers. One day, you may feel fed up with seeing it and decide, once and for all, to say adieu. Job done.

Unwanted Gifts

I was brought up to receive every gift graciously and happily, and rightly so. As a child, there do not seem to be too many problems associated with this: you play with the toys, read the books and wear the clothes. By the time you get older, a collection of gifts are clogging up your closet and the rest of your house. Even to this day, I accept whatever I am given with grace. I believe that people are giving you gifts with good intentions. I may try to give them hints as to what I would like to receive before a birthday or Christmas. If they get it wrong, I still accept the gift with gratitude and happiness. I don't wish to offend or hurt anybody's feelings by saying that their gift is not to my taste. So, I am faced with a small army of gifts I am reluctant to part with, out of respect for the giver.

I have recently come to the realisation that this situation is not helping anyone. So I now give these gifts away.

I would rather they made somebody else happy than sit around in my closet, just creating clutter. I grant you that it is not always an easy thing to do, especially when the giver is a person close to you. You don't want to appear ungrateful. If you can't do this, don't force it on yourself and feel guilty for it. This won't help you in any way.

Good luck to you. This is the one area that I have found to be the most difficult. The attachment, not to the object itself, but to the person who has given it to us, is the problem to overcome. Please let me know how you deal with this. I'd love to know.

Deal With Excuses

We all make excuses from time to time for not keeping our closet tidy. Examples we have seen are not having the time, the energy or the inclination.

These have not helped you tackle this mess up to now. They only enabled you to carry on making it worse. Take responsibility for the mess. There is no need and nothing to be gained by blaming anything or anyone for it. No need to come up with excuses.

The 'way to salvation' is to admit that your actions led your closet to this state. From now on, take responsibility to tidy up and clean as you go. You will feel happier doing it, if you feel that nobody else is to blame. The other positive is that, when it's all done, you can give yourself a big pat on the back and treat yourself. It was all thanks to you, after all.

Rather than allowing excuses to stop us from carrying out our tasks, let's reject them and find a solution.

Here are some examples of excuses and what we can do to combat them:

Lack of time

This is a favourite for most people. I once heard the concept of the 'irreducible minimum'. To those people who say they cannot spare any time at all, they should try the following.

Spare one minute only to do a task, any task. No-one can say that they cannot spare one minute, 60 seconds, of their time. Do this for a few days. You'll soon accept that you can spare one minute. In fact, you'll find that the one minute easily becomes five. If you can spare five minutes for any one task, try that for a few days. You'll quickly find that five minutes can become fifteen, twenty or even thirty. Once you have realised how much time you can free up, you'll be amazed at the things you can do with it. While working full-time, I managed to free up some 30 hours per week, to write my first book in the evenings and at weekends!

So, unless you are physically chained to a desk 24/7 or have an enormous family and no help, most people should be able to find some time, every day, to keep things tidy. Perhaps, you are like millions of people who watch between 20 to 35 hours of TV per week. If so, this means that you sit staring at a square box for 1.5 to almost 3 hours per day! Could you maybe spare some of this time to tidy up instead? It is amazing where it is possible to claw back a few minutes and what can be done even in that short time. If you really cannot miss any TV program, why not do tasks during the advert breaks? These seem longer and longer anyway, as much as five to six minutes at a time. Or, watch your programmes online, which incorporates less breaks and you can utilise that saved time to do your tasks. You can try to deal with one part of your closet at a time. Choose whether you want to clear out one shelf, one drawer or one side of the closet.

Let's see what can be done during the breaks.

- First TV break
- As soon as the adverts start, gather a few bags and cleaning products.

- Second break
- Take the above to your closet.

- Third break
- Empty the contents of your shelf or drawer onto your bed.

- Fourth break
- Clean the inside of the shelf or drawer.

- Fifth break
- Sort the contents out into various bags, as per the decluttering exercise.
- You may have to use more than one break.

- Other breaks
- Put everything that you are keeping in its rightful place.
- Put away the cleaning products and bags.

By the time your favourite shows are over and you go to bed, at least one part of your closet will be tidied up. You would have done some exercise too, if you had to run up and down the stairs during each break. You see, with a bit of discipline, you can achieve what you previously thought was not possible, due to lack of time.

The relevant question is never 'can you do it?' but always 'do you want to do it?'

Over committed

Finding time to do your own things, instead of rushing around to do urgent tasks can be difficult when you are in charge of a family, home or caring for sick or aged relatives.

Certainly, when you manage to have a few minutes to yourself, the last thing you want to do is sort out your closet. Instead, you just want to sit or lie there and breathe. Just do that and don't feel guilty about it. You deserve some rest.

I am not advocating that you should be constantly on the go.

As I've said before, there is an 'I' in 'tidy', so grab some 'you' time when needed.

I've already mentioned the concept of the irreducible minimum. It works just as well on the time scale of one year as it does for one day. You are bound to have one day in the year that you are not rushing around for everybody else and you feel inclined to declutter. That one day a year could turn into one day a month or even one day a week. All because you are suddenly looking for it. If you are looking after relatives or children, why not involve them? They may find it amusing and you might all have a good time. You may end up giving away some items to them and, because they are relatives, you don't have to dither too much on whether to give things away. Giving to family is so much easier.

Don't know how

With the advent of the internet, nobody can use the excuse 'I don't know how to do this'.

Within minutes or even seconds, you can find the answer to all your questions, and the solution to most of your problems. If you don't know, find out. Then do it.

No help

There is no use lamenting over a lack of help. The solution is to get help from your partner, children or friends, by offering rewards or turning the task into a game. If you still can't get any help, do not worry about the size of the job at hand. Just break it down into manageable chunks and do these as and when you can. Soon, the whole thing will be done.

Not my job

If everyone said this, nothing would be done. It's not your job? Take responsibility and make it your job.

Once you get the habit of being a doer, you may find that it spreads into other areas of your life. You may get a reputation at work for getting things done. This could lead to better pay, promotion or better prospects and more money to spend on nice clothes for your wardrobe.

It wasn't in today's horoscope

Tongue in cheek, I know, but to get out of doing something, we may resort to using any excuse, however lame it may be. This is the laziness habit rearing its head again.

You make excuses for not doing things because, although deep down you know you should, you just don't want to. This is the laziness habit.

The answer to this is action. Instead of deferring the task, take full responsibility and just do it. If you genuinely can't do it right now, set a definite date and commit to doing it on that date or before.

Once you commit, you will remove stress as well anger, guilt, and worry. Usually, the tasks you are afraid of tackling don't end up as bad as you make them out to be. How many times have you heard people say: "It was really nothing in the end, if I'd known it was going to be that easy, I'd have it done sooner?"

Stop the prevarication right now and decide once and for all to do all the things you've been putting off. Write down a list of all these jobs, small or large, and start ticking them off as you do them.

You will feel a huge sense of relief and achievement once they are completed. Treat yourself.

Everyone deserves the joy of satisfaction and a job well done.

Leave Room For Good Things

In Feng Shui, clutter is defined as:

'Anything that you do not use, do not love, or do not keep in an orderly manner'.

I am not a Feng Shui expert, but the above hits the spot. Anything that fits this definition should not be kept. Why fill our lives with unloved objects that sap our energy and wellbeing? It is better to get rid of these and replace them with things that we love and use.

Unloved and unworn clothes take up valuable space in your closet. When these are gone, you have made space for better clothes; clothes that will be cared for, loved and worn. This is what I hope. There is another important reason to declutter. It is not about acquiring more space but about your own wellbeing. Clutter is visually stressful and does not allow for rest and peaceful thinking.

Exercise

If you are reading this book before having decluttered, try this exercise now. It is a variation of the visualisation exercise you used to get you motivated in Chapter 5.

Think about your clutter.

Try to visualise the mess, clothes everywhere, nothing folded, all in disarray.

Better still, if you have not yet started to declutter, go into your room and see it in situ.

Look at all the clutter inside your closet.

Notice how it has spilled out from your closet.

It is now under your bed, on the floor and the windowsills.

Now, notice how you feel about it.

Do you feel calm, rested and relaxed?

Or do you feel stressed, unhappy and tired?

Now try to visualise your tidy closet.

All your clothes are neatly put away, sorted by your chosen system.

All hangers are the same colour, which adds to the harmonious look.

Notice how you feel about it.

Do you still feel stressed and tired?

Or, hopefully, do you now feel relaxed and happy?

Whether we want to admit it or not, clutter has the power to make us feel negative and tired. I have noticed this effect with relatives, friends and myself. I cannot think straight and I lack energy. Energy cannot flow as it is stopped at every turn. Once your clutter is cleared, you will notice a difference in your physical and emotional state because energy is able to circulate. The action of decluttering and the tidiness itself will improve your life for the better. Do try it and please let me know your experience.

Reminder: How To Keep It All Under Control

Here are some reminders to help you keep everything in check:

One in, one out: if you bring a new item in, remember to take one out, whether by giving or ditching. This may not work for you just after a big purge, but do try to do this as soon as you can and make it a habit. Remember that it only takes 30 consecutive days to form a habit!

Always put things away: do not allow one thing out of place or more will follow. Chaos soon reigns.

Keep your sorting system in place, whether by garment type and/or colour. It makes it easier to tidy things up as you have a system that works.

Your closet is the repository of all your beautiful clothes. Take pride in it.

Also, take pride in the clothes you wear. They have the power to make you look and feel great. Appreciate them.

Appreciate every item of clothing you own. If you can't find anything nice to say about it, isn't it time to give it away to someone who will appreciate it?

Try not to get too attached to things as it will be difficult to get rid of them when the time comes.

Keep a charity box at hand. Make yourself put one item in it per day. It is a win-win for all: good for you, good for charity.

For those of you who really have trouble letting go of your clothes and can't decide whether to keep them or donate them, keep a large box in the garage or by the front door. Put in this box clothes you dither about. Now and again, take a piece out and wear it. If you feel and look good in it, keep it. If, however, after a reasonable amount of time, those clothes have not been worn, it is safe to say that they never will be. You can now donate them. Decision made.

Commit to keeping everything in order. Do your best not to break this promise.

Take 100% responsibility: no more excuses!

Stay positive and keep smiling. Isn't life beautiful?

As a reward for seeing your project through to the end, I am offering you a bonus chapter on essentials and classics for your wardrobe. You can also read my other books for more detailed advice. Thank you for staying with me.

BONUS CHAPTER 10

WARDROBE ESSENTIALS

"Each individual piece is a calculated attempt to entice women to add to their wardrobe." - Bill Blass

I couldn't end this book without helping you to organise your wardrobe even further. So, I wrote this free chapter for you on the essential and classic pieces to have and keep in your closet. These pieces will give you plenty of mileage and will not let you down. Lamenting that you have nothing to wear will be a thing of the past, thanks to my advice and tips. Some of you may already be familiar with these, while many of you will welcome a list of classic items that will complete an essential wardrobe.

Classics

Before I give you the list, a few words about classics. As we have seen earlier, keep only what fits you, what suits you and what you love. However, if you always want to look chic and well put together, a mainly classic wardrobe will keep you in good stead.

Classics last longer than trendy pieces as they are versatile and can be worn on most occasions. They have a good cut and style, which make them stand out. Due to their versatility, you don't have to buy many pieces.

The same item can be worn with many others. You may wear a classic piece once a week as opposed to wearing a trendy piece twice in a season and then never again.

Even though I suggest going for classics of a good quality, it does not mean that you have to treble your clothes budget. By waiting for seasonal reductions, you will end up paying the same amount as for low quality items, or even less.

My own wardrobe consists of quality clothes, mainly classics. I assure you that most of these were bought at reduced prices.

I, like all women, enjoy window shopping, looking through clothes rails in expensive shops and generally browsing. So, when the sales arrive, I know exactly what to buy and where to buy it. No more expensive mistakes. Unless I specifically need an item right away, I prefer to wait. This way, I keep to my modest budget, yet it allows me to afford better clothes. By quality, I don't mean 'designer'. To me, it would seem ridiculous to pay £100 for a T-shirt. I don't care which designer it is from.

A T-shirt is a T-shirt. You can look just as good in a £20 T-shirt from the High Street. Classics and quality do not mean designer and do not mean logos either. Classics mean understatement and elegance. Classics do not mean ostentatiousness. You do not have to be wealthy to wear quality classics and dress well. You can see just as many wealthy women in dreadful designer clothes as women on lower budgets who dress with good taste and style.

I regularly write posts on classics and what to wear on my blog. Visit it now and again to get your eye in.

What To Keep According To Your Body Shape

Knowing what to wear according to your shape is tantamount to being well dressed. If you are still unsure about what suits your figure, check out my book entitled 'Plus Size'. This book gives plenty of advice, for larger ladies, on clothes suitable for the five main body shapes, rectangle, pear, apple, hourglass and inverted triangle.

As a quick guide, see below for the main characteristics of clothes that do most for the various shapes.

Rectangle

Pieces that:

- Give you a feminine shape
- Give you a waist
- Boost your bust and bottom
- Boost your cleavage, such as V-necks
- Are belted, such as jackets
- Emphasise your feminine assets, such as pencil, A line and full skirts.

Pear

Pieces that:

- Boost your bust and widen your upper body
- Have detailing along the top, arms and towards the face
- Cinch at the waist
- Are light coloured above the waist and dark below.

Apple

Pieces that:

- Show off your cleavage, arms and legs

- Are not tight at the waist.

Inverted Triangle

Pieces that:

- Are simple in design for your upper torso

- Widen you up below the waist, such as A line skirts

- Are dark above the waist and light below.

Hourglass

Pieces that:

- Are cinched at the waist

- Emphasise your feminine figure, such as pencil skirts

- Show off your cleavage.

The following essentials are what I deem to be classics that work.

White Buttoned-Down Blouse Or Shirt

Unless you have to wear them every day for work, only a couple of these will do. Stop buying any more. If you choose to own only two, you can have one short-sleeved and one long-sleeved one. That is all you really need, if your washing is done regularly.

♥ Tip

White buttoned down blouses or shirts should be fitted and go in at the waist to flatter your figure, whether you are slim or plus-sized.

Do not buy them square shaped and loose or this is what you will look like.

Remember the 'wow' factor?

Little Black Dress

Your LBD should be fitted and skim your body. It should not be too tight or it will show all your lumps and bumps. On the other hand, it can't be too loose or it will give you a shapeless silhouette and make you look larger than you are. Unless you are apple shaped, your dress should be fitted at the waist. A colourful belt will add interest.

The choice is yours when it comes to LBDs, as long as you follow simple guidelines. They can be sleeveless or with short, mid or long sleeves. Knee length (just above, at or just below) is the most flattering and elegant length for all women, regardless of size, shape or age.

Try to have at least one black dress as you will never regret having the versatility of this colour in your wardrobe. It can literally be worn for every occasion, depending on the accessories you choose. Once you have at least one black dress, try other colours. The classic and more versatile colours are navy, red, grey and white. Be careful with other colours or tones as they can be 'in' one year and 'out' the next. By keeping to basic colours, you ensure that they are always fashionable and become true classics.

As stated earlier, they look best fitted and

skimming the body. The pencil and A-line are the most wearable styles.

Bandeau style, also known as body-con, being too tight and restrictive, will create unsightly bulges when you sit down, unless you are ultra slim and toned. However, being cut far too close to the body, a bandeau dress will not be deemed a classic.

Any neckline is fine as long as it does not reveal too much cleavage.

Wear LBDs with the following:

- Little cardigans
- Sweaters
- Short jackets
- Bolero jackets
- Knee length or long coats
- Shawls

Wear your little black dress with flat, medium or high heeled shoes in the colour you wish, either matching, contrasting or nude.

In winter, it can be worn with black leather, high heeled boots. Black fishnet or patterned tights or stockings will add a touch of sexiness without being overt. A hint of fishnet being revealed at the knee is enough. A hint always has more effect than going the whole hog. Keep them guessing.

A bit of mystery is sexy. Showing too much is not.

One last thing. Avoid pairing your LBD with coloured tights. They do not flatter legs at all. There is something ghastly about aubergine or bright green legs. Beware!

LBD for Rectangles

Go for fitted pieces with a belt to give you shape and curves. Detailing at the neckline will help. Pencil and A line dresses will look smashing on you.

LBD for Pears

The most flattering LBD for Pear shapes will be one that showcases your waistline and slimmer upper body. You should choose one with an attractive neckline with detailing at the torso area and/or on the sleeves. The best style of skirt for Pears is the A line. A two-tone dress, light at the top, dark at the bottom, would be fabulous, if you could get your hands on one.

LBD for Apples

Apple shaped women have a rounded middle so they should wear a belt higher than their natural waistline with their LBD, but only if they are fairly slim. If not, choose to omit the belt altogether for a more flattering look.

Deflect attention away from your tummy area, either towards your gorgeous legs in amazing shoes, or towards your cleavage with a statement necklace or interesting neckline.

LBD for Inverted Triangles

Avoid boat and horizontal necklines as they widen your shoulders even further.

Opt for V necks instead, paired with A line skirts, in order to bring fullness to your lower area.

LBD for Hourglass

Any piece that showcases your feminine proportions is perfect for you.

So go for belted waistlines, pencil and A line style.

Striped Tops

This is a quintessentially French look. Breton tops are always 'in'. whatever the season or year.

I always have striped tops in my wardrobe. I have vests, as well as short and long sleeved tops. My favourites are, of course, navy and white stripes. They are versatile and have that 'ever so classic' look. They are easy to wear with white, red or blue trousers and those 'wear with anything' jeans. To retain the classic French look, throw on a jacket or blazer.

Black Trousers

Everyone, whatever their style, shape and size needs these for work, staying in or going out. They are a true staple in any woman's wardrobe. They can be worn with virtually any top, of any style and colour. I would advise against trousers with gathered pleats at the waist. They have a tendency to add bulk to the tummy.

Without wanting to sound funny, it is a sensitive area we all want to flatter and flatten, not fatten. Go for flat-fronted trousers instead.

Cardigans

The little fine ones are my absolute favourites, especially in super soft cashmere. They can be worn open over dresses, skirts and trousers to reveal a sexy, silk camisole or a printed blouse underneath. Worn buttoned up, they double up as a sweater. Shorter length ones are perfect with dresses. You can keep to the basic colours or go on trend. This will bring any classic outfit up to date. Longer and bulkier cardigans do not look as dressy, although they do have their uses.

Trench Coat

A good quality trench can be worn for mild rainy days, during spring and autumn. By choosing a reputable brand, this timeless classic will last you forever.

Black Suit

For office work, job interviews, formal meetings and occasions, dark suits are absolutely de rigueur. My favourites are skirt and dress suits as I enjoy looking feminine. Knee length is best for the skirt or dress and the style should be pencil or A-line. The neckline of the dress has to be high to remain professional and the jacket should be fitted at the waist, if possible.

For a more flattering look, long and loose jackets should be avoided. If you have to wear a suit every day, three suits should be enough for a regular rotation and dry cleaning, especially if you like to look different every day. Wearing different blouses, tops, jewellery, belts and shoes will do the trick. Court shoes in a medium heel are the most popular style, both for comfort and versatility. In winter, do not forget the slim knee-high boots, which will add a 'je ne sais quoi' to your skirt and dress suits.

♥ Tip

Avoid wearing navy with black, for instance a navy blouse with a black suit or black shirt with a navy skirt. These two colours are too close in tone to make an impact. They will blend in with each other. A fashion fail!

♥ Tip

Shoes with pointed toes look smart, sharp and chic when worn with trousers. The triangle peeking out from under the trouser leg will help elongate the foot and therefore the leg.

♥ Tip

Pear shaped women may find it difficult to find trousers that fit their small waist and larger derrière. The simple thing to do is to find trousers that fit at the bottom and thighs. Remember, suit trousers should absolutely not be tight. The waistline will probably be too large but you can have the waistline tailored. Et voilà, a perfect pair of trousers!

♥ Tip

Do not hesitate to wear coloured or patterned belts with skirts, dresses and trousers. Use thin silver, gold or snake-look belts to take your style up a notch. They will not only showcase your waistline but also brighten up your outfits and add an individual touch.

Dark-Wash Jeans

Whether you are slim or not, faded jeans are not in the least flattering. I find they make you look untidy and unkempt, and wider too.

For a classic look, you cannot go wrong with dark-wash denim jeans. These slim you down, thanks to their dark tone. They look clean and smart. You can dress them up or down, with a simple printed shirt or cream silk blouse. Flats or heels? It's up to you. Enjoy yourself and have fun.

Little Black Jacket

These jackets are cut short, more or less fitted and are usually square cut, à la Chanel.

They can be worn with your LBDs, skirts, trousers or even jeans, indeed most things.

Dressed up or down, they always look fabulous and can turn a plain outfit into a chic one in mere seconds.

Worn with pearls or a statement necklace, they will last you forever.

I have been wearing mine every single year

of the twelve years that I have owned it.

Whether this look is 'in' or not, I always receive compliments about it. You will too, once you get your lucky hands on this classic baby.

Quality Coat

A coat in a good quality fabric, such as wool or cashmere, will last and look fantastic for a number of winters. It will also keep you much warmer than cotton or manmade polyester blends ever could.

A long length gives you more versatility to team with knee length and longer dresses and skirts. It will give your legs more coverage on cold days too. Black, navy, grey, camel or cream are classic colours for winter coats.

Straight cut and military styles are classic shapes that never seem to date. Belted styles give you an hourglass shape instead of a square and boxy one.

Single breasted styles are the most flattering for all shapes and sizes. I am not a fan of 'cocoon' coats, which widen you at the middle, exactly the place where many women have a problem. I prefer the styles that give you a great figure.

Investing in a good cut, style and quality is a must, as a coat will be your outerwear for weeks and months on end. This is THE piece of clothing that you will wear every day in winter. Make sure that it makes you look good.

♥ Tip

Hang a full-length mirror by your front door. This way, you will be able to see your whole ensemble, just before you leave the house.

Shoes

The amount of shoes women have in their closet varies, but it is probably safe to say that we have far too many. If we are honest with ourselves, can we justify having many pairs of each style and colour?

Now that I apply a set system and question my purchases, my shoes no longer sit on a shelf, just looking pretty. Instead, they work hard for a living as they are worn regularly. That is what they were made for, to be worn, not act as knick-knacks and gather dust.

The list of shoes below are my recommendations. They are comfortable and will make you look chic and well put together. They are the finishing touch to any ensemble.

Boots

They should be knee high, in black or brown, with either low or high heels.

Knee high boots slim down the silhouette and are more flattering to the leg than shorter boots. Worn over skinny jeans or with skirts and dresses, they truly are a winter staple.

Booties

They can be black or grey, with a mid or high heel.

They look more feminine and dressier than low heeled booties, which can look a tad frumpy

Courts

In black or nude with a mid-heel, they are the essential shoes par excellence.

Professional yet feminine, they will see you through the day for work, job interviews, lunches, dinner, and many other occasions.

Due to their sheer versatility and high rate of wear, you will have to buy new ones more often than other styles.

Evening sandals

These obviously need to be dressy as they are for formal evening wear. In silver, gold or black, with a high heel, you will look fabulous.

Metallic sandals are extremely flattering and will suit most styles and colours of gowns, while black sandals are a favourite fail-safe.

Summer sandals

You only really need to have one pair, preferably in brown, with a flat or low heel. One pair is enough, although through heavy use during the summer, you may have to buy another pair next year. Choose them ultra comfortable, for your feet will be bare in them.

Stilettos

You need one or two pairs that make you feel ultra sexy and glamorous. In any colour, pattern or style, stilettos are to be cherished, due to their sexiness factor. As you are still supposed to walk and stand in them, ensure that the heel is not ridiculously vertiginous.

Platforms and wedges

One or two pairs may be enough in any colour or style, as long as they are comfortable and tasteful. These should come with a health warning, due to the risks of twisted ankles that can occur when the sole is extra high.

Some styles can also make your feet really clumpy and hoof-like, so choose wisely.

Ballet flats

These have been firm favourites of French women for decades, as they look more chic than sneakers.

You can be frivolous in colours and detailing if you wish, as long as you get the wear out of them.

Ensure that they offer sufficient arch and heel support to wear all day long.

Slippers

I know that they're not shoes per se but they are better than walking around the house barefoot and cracking your heels.

Lingerie Essentials

There is something really special about shoes. The same can be said about lingerie. I adore it!

Lingerie has so much power to make women feel beautiful and sexy. Sensuous silk, delicate lace, discreet ribbons, soft muted colours, exquisite detailing, all these go towards making us feel ultra special.

French women can't do without quality lingerie and do not mind spending large amounts on special pieces.

Silk chemises, sexy camisoles, bras and panties are all chosen with care.

The thing with lingerie is that you don't always buy it because you need it but because you succumb to the beauty of it.

That is ok in my book. The difficult thing to do when you get home though is to get rid of one item you already have, to make room for this one. I don't think that this rule was meant for lingerie.

Wouldn't you agree that there is always enough room for one new pair of silk panties in your drawer?

Oh là là.

Less Is More

Try to adopt the 'less is more' approach. Here are a few examples of this concept.

The less stuff I have, the more space I gain.

The less I spend on trendy pieces that will hardly be worn, the more money I'll have for quality pieces.

The less time I waste finding things to wear in the mornings, the more time I'll have for breakfast.

The less clutter I've got, the calmer I'll be.

The less stressed I am, due to my mess, the happier my family will be.

The less I dither about decluttering, the more tidying up I will be able to do.

The less ruffles my outfit has, the classier I shall look.

Creating Outfits Easily

Finally, here is an easy way to create outfits.

We have established that once your closet is purged or decluttered of all the unnecessary stuff, you will be left with only pieces that work for you and your lifestyle.

The more classic and unfussy pieces you have, the easier it will be to create outfits. A good habit to develop is to buy only items that will work with as many other pieces as possible. Before creating an outfit, first choose the main piece. This way, it is easier to select the secondary items to go with it.

Let's say, you want to wear your navy skirt.

Lay it on your bed.

Go through your tops, blouses and shirts. It is now easy because they are sorted by colour and garment type. Pick the one you want (white, red, cream or striped for instance), and lay it down on the bed above the skirt, so that you can see how these two work together.

The belt could already be hung with the skirt so you don't have to find one. If belts are stored in a box, bring out the whole box and look through it. Keeping them all in one place makes it easier to find one.

Pick a jacket, jewellery and underwear. Lay out all your pieces on the bed.

You spend less time trying things on and removing them, as you can see at a glance if the outfit works or not. This is a fast way of creating an outfit. The fact that you don't have too many pieces in your closet works in your favour as it gives you less choice. Thus it helps you to reach a quicker decision.

It is much easier to choose one top from a choice of five than it is from a choice of 15 or more. This way, you will save time and not run out of patience. You will look better dressed too. As you have kept only clothes that look good and work together, your outfit is less likely to look odd and out of place.

♥ Tip

Create outfits with your clothes and photograph them. You can either wear them and take a 'selfie', put them on a mannequin or lay them on the bed. Include accessories, handbag and shoes for a full outfit. Pin these photos on the inside of your closet doors. They will act as inspiration for when you run out of ideas and want to get dressed quickly.

♥ Tip

Cut out magazine pictures of your favourite icon, fashion model or Hollywood star in outfits you like and which would look great on you. As above, tack these on the inside of your closet doors. Alternatively, keep them in a special file on your computer for inspiration.

That's it. You have finished the book. The Tidy Closet is yours. Felicitations!

CONCLUSION

We have examined your current situation and given a cursory glance at the psychology behind cluttering. You now know the differences between a clutterer and a hoarder and concluded that you are most likely the former rather than the latter.

You discovered the disadvantages of clutter

and benefits of a tidy closet. You can't wait to reap those benefits for yourself.

You got motivated into starting your own decluttering. You now know the power of active words, visualisation, friends and last but not least, sweet little rewards.

I gave you simple and clear steps to go through, to break the task down into manageable chunks.

Organisation and storage solutions were presented to you, as ideas to implement if you so wish.

Wardrobe organisation came next. You learned the systems you can use for your benefit.

Towards the end, in Keeping Up The Good Work, you were given tools to help carry on after the decluttering.

The last chapter was a bonus for you, a final gift to those who would like help in creating a classic wardrobe for their tidy closet.

You were given extra tips and simple exercises throughout the book, which were designed to be fun.

I hope you have found the motivation and know-how to start your own decluttering project. All you really need is a clear goal of what you want to achieve and the willpower to get it done. You now know that there is no point in making excuses. It is all go from here on. Well done. The Tidy Closet can be yours. Please let me know how you get on.

OTHER BOOKS BY THE AUTHOR

How To Be Chic and Elegant: Tips From A French Woman

How To Be Chic and Elegant is fast becoming a cult classic.

Marie-Anne Lecoeur gives you over 200 simple tips in this book that will propel you to sidewalk model in no time at all.

Here are just a few of the subjects covered:

The principles of French elegance

The secrets of achieving a French Woman's style

Over 200 tips to attain that chic look

Which clothes to avoid at all costs

Many women are crying out for the secrets of effortless French chic. Here, in one small book, you have those secrets and more besides. This book is direct and straightforward, with no waffle or padding. Apply the tips right away, and literally see results in the mirror immediately. Save money on impulse purchases and learn to sharpen your style eye.

Follow this French author's simple instructions and start hearing the compliments roll in!

How To Be Chic & Elegant: Plus Size

Are you plus sized or even just a bit overweight?

Are you fed up of buying the wrong clothes for your shape?

Do you want to look chic and elegant from now on?

If yes, then look no further: This book is tailored for you!

The fashion industry and most style authors assume that all plus sized women are the same shape. Wrong!

French author Marie-Anne Lecoeur acknowledges that plus sized women also come in different shapes.

The advice in each chapter of this book is carefully tailored to the five main body shapes: Apple, Pear, Hourglass, Inverted Triangle and Rectangle.

From the foundations of shapewear to clothes and accessories, Marie-Anne Lecoeur gives detailed and specific assistance to help you transform your sense of style forever.

Why wait any longer? Make the most of your figure and look sensational today!

Pear Shape: Daywear Mini-Guide

Not sure how to make the most of your shape?

Don't know your do's from your don'ts?

At a loss about choosing what to wear?

If you do not know which clothes will make you look fabulous and which won't, this pear shape mini-guide will show you.

French author Marie-Anne Lecoeur shows you how you can attain the chic and elegance that French women seem to exude.

Pear Shape is direct and to the point, with no waffle or extra padding.

You will no longer waste your hard-earned cash on clothes that do not work for you. You will discover how to choose the right clothes for your shape.

Here are just a few of the many questions answered:

Which popular item should not be worn by pears?

Which past decade is pear-licious, and why?

Why avoiding this feature will make you lose inches on your hips and bottom?

Do not let your shape stop you from becoming the new chic and elegant you!

BEFORE YOU GO

I hope that this book has inspired and motivated you to get on with your decluttering. If you have enjoyed the advice and tips given, kindly consider writing a review on Amazon. Positive reviews give authors the encouragement they need to continue writing.

Merci beaucoup.

ILLUSTRATIONS

Introduction/Conclusion p1 and p177
© Can Stock Photo Inc. / Aleutie

The Psychology Behind Clutter p7
© Can Stock Photo Inc. / katarinka

The Situation Now p25
© Can Stock Photo Inc. / V_Gri

The Disadvantages of Clutter p31
© Can Stock Photo Inc. / Kakigori

The Benefits Of A Tidy Closet p41
© Can Stock Photo Inc. / lian2011

Get Motivated! p49
© Can Stock Photo Inc. / MiraBavutti

Step By Step: Let's Do It! p61
© Can Stock Photo Inc. / katarinka

Organization And Storage Ideas p89
© Can Stock Photo Inc. / ponytail1414

Organising Your Wardrobe p101
© Can Stock Photo Inc. / ponytail1414

Keep Up The Good Work p121
© Can Stock Photo Inc. / gurza

Wardrobe Essentials p151
© Can Stock Photo Inc. / intararit

MAR 0 3 2015

CPSIA information can be obtained at www.ICGtesting.com
Printed in the USA
LVOW10s0924091114

412747LV00012B/394/P